QUEEN of The BLUES

QUEEN of The BLUES
A Biography of Dinah Washington

JIM HASKINS

William Morrow and Company, Inc.   New York

Copyright © 1987 by Jim Haskins

"I Don't Hurt Anymore" by Jack Rollins and Don Robertson
Copyright 1953, 1954 by Hill & Range Songs, Inc.
Copyrights and all rights assigned to Unichappell Music, Inc.
(Rightsong Music, Publisher)
International Copyright Secured
ALL RIGHTS RESERVED
Used by permission

Library of Congress Cataloging-in-Publication Data

Haskins, James, 1941–
  Queen of the blues.

  Discography: p.
  Includes index.
  1. Washington, Dinah, 1924–1963.   2. Singers—
United States—Biography.   I. Title.
ML420.W2H37   1987   784.5'3'00924 [B]   86-23686
ISBN 0-688-04846-3

Printed in the United States of America

First Edition

1 2 3 4 5 6 7 8 9 10

BOOK DESIGN BY JAYE ZIMET

To Kathy

ACKNOWLEDGMENTS

I AM grateful to all the people who shared their memories and mementos of Dinah Washington, in particular LaRue Manns. Others to whom I am deeply indebted are, in alphabetical order, Gordon Austin, Patti Austin, Ruth Bowen, Eddie Chamblee, Jimmy Cobb, Charles Davis, Leonard Feather, Ferris Kimbrough, Dick "Night Train" Lane, Ernestine McClendon, Evelyn Parker, Slappy White, and Jack Wilson. Irving Ashby, Buddy Collette, Bill Greene, and Lionel Hampton also gave important information. Gene Grissom provided an extremely helpful listing of Dinah's recording dates, places, and personnel, as did Polygram Records.

Halimah Brooks gave valuable assistance tracking people down and conducting interviews, as did Kathy Benson. Patricia Allen-Browne helped in transcribing tapes and doing library research, and Ann Kalkhoff and Mark Gridley provided additional research help. Libraries whose collections proved most helpful included the Jazz Institute at Rutgers University, the Library for the Performing Arts at Lincoln Center, and the Schomburg Center for Research in Black Culture.

CONTENTS

Of Music and Men

DINAH Washington's first husband was John Young. His name notwithstanding, he was considerably older than she —in his thirties or forties, according to LaRue Manns, Dinah's longtime friend and companion. Dinah was still in high school at the time, but experienced beyond her years. John Young was only one of many men she tried to interest during those years, for she was woefully unhappy at home and anxious to get away. "He talked my language," she recalled years later, "and said he would help me get into show business. . . . I was seventeen and absolutely dumb about the ways of the world. But seizing the opportunity to get away from home, like many other women have done, I married him."

Home, at the time, was Chicago's South Side ghetto, and, according to Manns, Dinah's family was very poor. In addition to Dinah and her brother, Harold, there were two very young girls named Estrellita and Clarissa, children by Dinah's mother's second marriage, which had not lasted. Dinah's family were learning that up North things like marriage had a way of not lasting.

Dinah, had been born in Tuscaloosa, Alabama, in August 1924. There is some question as to the actual date of her birth, which is given in various sources as the eighth, the twenty-second, and the twenty-ninth. The births of black babies were frequently not recorded in the South then, and Dinah probably did not have a birth certificate until she needed one to get married or to get a passport. Gordon Austin, who knew her well in the 1940s and 1950s, recalls that she was a Leo (about July 20 to August 20) and believes that her personality was true to the sign: "She wanted to be the boss. She was good to people, but she wanted control. What she needed most was a good friend, someone who would be with her and agree with her on her things, but also be firm with her. And there had to be a lot of respect between them. With men, at least, she never found that."

In her early years, Dinah, who was christened Ruth Jones (for the sake of clarity, she is called Dinah here), didn't have much contact with men. Her father, Ollie Jones, was a small-time gambler who was often gone for weeks or months at a time. Her mother, Alice Williams Jones, was a domestic, who also had to leave her children often to go out to work. Dinah did have her brother, Harold, for company, but a sibling was no replacement for parents in her eyes. From the time she was three or four years old, Dinah remembered being very lonely and being afraid of loneliness.

It is significant that Dinah should date her loneliness to the age of three or four, because she was about that age when her family moved to Chicago, joining the postwar migration of blacks north to the urban centers that promised not only jobs but a measure of dignity as well. They probably chose Chicago because other family members had already made the trek and could help them get started; but they might also have chosen Chicago because it was on the Illinois Central Line or because as Arnold Shaw suggests in his book *Honkers and Shouters,* the *Chicago Defender,* read by blacks all over the country, urged southern blacks to come with slogans like "If you can freeze to death in the North and be free, why freeze to death in the South and be a slave?" Chicago was a magnet for blacks from the South; between 1910 and 1930 almost two hundred thousand migrated to that city, turning the South Side into one of the largest black ghettos in the nation.

Following closely behind the people came their institutions, most particularly the church, and by the time Dinah's family arrived there, the South Side was dotted with Baptist storefront churches and holiness and spiritual temples where they could worship and find the sense of community that they had enjoyed in the South. Accompanying the migrants, too, were the sporting-life institutions—bars and jook joints, brothels and pool halls—that served as a kind of escape mechanism for despair for those who did not find solace in the church; they attracted a white clientele as well. These existed side by side with the churches and temples, and a little girl skipping along the street with a hymn in her heart might just be interrupted by the sound of a honky-tonk piano or a throaty blues. The pull of these diametrically opposed institutions was evident in Dinah's own family, where her father was not a churchgoer and her mother was holier-than-thou. It was an opposition that they'd been able to keep under control back in Tuscaloosa, but once they got to Chicago, there were fewer community ties to keep their problems at bay. The Great Depression descended upon the South Side like the heel of a heavy boot, and Ollie Jones was more often out of work than not and more often gone than at home. Eventually he left home altogether and though he maintained contact with the family, he could not be counted on for either emotional or financial support. "They were living in the projects," says LaRue Manns, "and there were rats and roaches and they didn't have enough food or enough clothes to wear."

Before little Dinah started school, she didn't realize that

all families were not as poor as hers. Far more significant to her young mind were her mother's abiding faith and constant cautions that Dinah stay off the street and away from bad neighborhood children. Significant, too, apparently, was her mother's criticism of her, for Dinah never in her life believed that her mother really loved her. Once Dinah started school, she came to realize that there was an economic hierarchy in the world and that she and her family were at the bottom. She knew who was poor and who wasn't and that such things were identified by who had a different dress to wear to church than to school, who had shoes without holes in the soles, who had lots of presents at Christmastime. Dinah knew that she was poor and was ashamed. She was ashamed, too, of being from the South, an origin of which native and less newly arrived Chicagoans never tired of reminding Dinah and others like her. And so young Dinah soon realized that her southern way of speaking also placed her at the bottom of the social hierarchy in Chicago's black community, at the top of which were the native Chicagoans and the light-skinned blacks, who looked down on the poor, dark-skinned recent immigrants from the South as if they were dirty and smelled bad. She had yet even to come into contact with white people.

Dinah had bad skin as a child and suffered with the nickname Alligator. She was also chubby. There was little about herself of which she could be proud, except for her musical talent. From an early age, Dinah showed great talent at the piano and at singing. In addition to working as a domestic, Alice Jones played piano at Saint Luke's Baptist Church for a little extra money. She also gave lessons, in particular to her daughter. While still in elementary school, Dinah was playing piano at the church, and by the time she was an adolescent, she and her mother, who was no slouch as a singer herself, had discovered that she could sing. Her sweet, high-voiced renditions of gospel songs endeared her

to the congregation, and she became a local prodigy, in
great demand at area churches. For a time, she and her
mother performed as a duo, each taking her turn playing
the piano and singing. However, her mother quickly realized
that it was her daughter's talent that might be parlayed into
something, and she began to coach her. Mama Jones realized
that Dinah was the main attraction, because of her youth
and the great clarity of her voice. It was she who imbued
in her daughter the sense of the living presence of God that
elevated her singing to the level of the sacred. But it was
also she who held God over her daughter like a club and
who caused young Dinah to feel that whatever she did was
not good enough in the eyes of her mother, and by extension,
in the eyes of God.

In the meantime, however, Dinah's minor success as a
gospel singer in local churches had done much for her standing among her peers. "Even in high school the girls liked
her [singing]," recalls musician Eddie Chamblee, who married Dinah more than a quarter of a century later. "We boys
weren't too interested. Should have been." Walter Grayson,
son of the pastor of Saint Luke's Baptist Church, kind of
liked her. But the girls were most admiring, and at least
with her girlfriends Dinah began to come out of her shell
and to feel that she was worthy.

Dinah made little or no money singing gospel in churches.
The family still lived in grinding poverty. "She and her
mother had to share one pair of stockings," says LaRue
Manns. "She had to wash out her mother's pair of stockings
to wear if she was going someplace, you know, and her
mother wasn't going." Memories of that kind of hardship
stayed with her. Years later, Dinah insisted on having only
the best, and she always had plenty of stockings. Manns
recalls, "I used to ask her, 'Why do you buy so many
stockings at one time?' She said, 'Number one, you tear
'em, and number two, I want plenty of stockings. I don't

ever want to have to wear somebody else's stockings.' "

Dinah was bitter about being poor, and after a time she began to wonder if she couldn't become equally successful in an area of music where she could make some money. The Chicago of that time was alive with jazz and blues, due not only to its location as a crossroads in the Midwest but also to the 1917 closing of Storyville, the red-light district of New Orleans, and the resultant migration of a number of New Orleans jazzmen to the Windy City. By the 1920s, the city was a major radio center and thereby attracted even more fine jazz musicians. The high school Dinah attended, Wendell Phillips High at Thirty-ninth and Calumet, was a veritable cradle of jazz, producing over the years such notables as Eddie South, Ray Nance, Hayes Alvis, Happy Cauldwell, Milt Hinton, and Nat King Cole. Through her peers, Dinah also learned about such singers as Billie Holiday, who became her idol in the secular field. Recalls Jack Wilson, who played piano with her in the late fifties and early sixties, "She told me that when she was a kid going to school in Chicago, she heard that Billie Holiday was coming to Chicago and was going to land at Midway Airport. Dinah skipped school to go to the airport and see Billie get off the plane. This was when Billie was at her height and always wearing ermine and carrying those two little dogs. And Dinah had all her records and just idolized her, and she said that when she saw Billie step off that plane, she thought that Billie was the most beautiful woman she had ever seen.'' Thus, Dinah was strongly pulled to secular music, but her mother was firmly against her going outside the church or singing any of the sinful music that filled the streets of the South Side. So, Dinah began to sing popular songs without her mother's knowledge. It was easy to do so at school, where her singing ability brought her the popularity she longed for. At age fifteen, also without her mother's knowledge, she entered a talent contest at the Regal

Theater; she sang "I Can't Face the Music" and won. This brought her to the attention of local club owners, and for several months Dinah, using a different name so that her mother would not find out, sang in the secular venues of which her mother disapproved. She told her mother that she was going to sing at various churches and she continued to do just enough church work to keep her mother from knowing what she was doing on the side. Trumpet player Walter Fuller remembered that in 1940 she performed at the new Grand Terrace, a venerable Chicago jazz club that had moved locations, in the same show in which he appeared with his very short-lived big band. It is unlikely, however, that she could have kept her double life from her mother for long, and so it was fortunate for her that she was discovered by Sallie Martin.

Martin was a gospel singer who had made her debut in 1932 at Ebenezer Baptist Church in Chicago with Thomas A. Dorsey, a former blues pianist who had gone into gospel and sparked a revolution in that form of music. Together, they trained gospel choruses all over Chicago and by 1933 were traveling to other cities in the Midwest and in the South to organize gospel choruses. By 1937, Dorsey's University Gospel Singers were broadcasting over Chicago's WLFL, and soon after that Dorsey and Martin formed the Gospel Singers Convention. Success apparently spoiled the relationship, and in 1940 Martin and Dorsey split up, leaving Martin on her own. She didn't have the money to support a traveling chorus, so she decided to experiment with a solo act. She hired the young Dinah not as a singer but as her accompanist, although there was no question that Dinah could also sing.

Not only did she have an exceptional voice, she also had flawless diction, which, considering her milieu, was also exceptional. No one taught her diction; she taught herself, by listening to records. "Dinah believed that people should understand what you're talking about when you're singing,'' says Ruth Bowen, a longtime friend and Dinah's agent in her later years. ''She taught herself, by listening. Dinah spoke beautifully, just normally so.'' Perhaps she also taught herself by going to Bette Davis movies, for Jimmy Cobb, who worked with her for years and was her boyfriend for about three of them, is convinced that she was strongly influenced by Bette Davis, to whom she was only exposed through movies.

By the time Dinah joined Sallie Martin, she was sixteen and anxious to be featured on the stage. Realizing that having a young prodigy like Dinah would help attract audiences, Martin had no objection to her singing. In fact, she encouraged it. But Dinah was hard to handle. As Martin told Tony Heilbut, author of *The Gospel Sound,* ''She could really sing but, shoot, she'd catch the eye of some man and she'd be out the church before the minister finished off the doxology.'' Nevertheless, Martin kept Dinah on, and the teenager was a member of the first all-woman gospel group that Martin founded, the Sallie Martin Colored Ladies Quartet. Traveling around with Martin brought Dinah into contact with a number of other gospel singers, among them Mahalia Jackson, the Reverend C. L. Franklin, father of Aretha and a gospel star in his own right, and Roberta Martin, who was her favorite. ''I remember coming to a national Gospel singers' convention in Brooklyn, and that was really something to hear,'' Dinah told Leonard Feather of *Down Beat* years later. ''To me, Roberta Martin is the greatest. She started that fad of the Gospel sound on the piano. She taught me piano, and she had a group called the Martin Singers.'' During that time, Dinah came to love gospel people, as a group, and she would keep up her membership in the Gospel Singers Convention for the rest of her life, though after she turned to secular music, they wouldn't allow her to sing at these conventions. She learned a great deal from traveling with Sallie Martin, particularly about professionalism—about singing her heart out for a group of ten as well as for a church filled with hundreds—and about the importance of recording. During the time she was with Martin, Martin formed a gospel publishing company whose first publication, "Just a Closer Walk with Thee," was highly successful. But after about two years, Dinah decided that gospel singing just wasn't for her. She hated the utter noncommercialism of it, not knowing what she was going to get paid because first they would sing and then they would sit through a free-will offering, which she found humiliating. Then, too, she found the social milieu too restrictive. Sallie Martin sounded too much like her mother when she warned, "There isn't but one thing that I say will keep us back and that is singing one thing and then doing so different when you get out of your service, that will really hinder anybody." And, "You've got to live right, and if you're not right, you need to get right." Dinah had her own ideas about getting right, and they had to do with getting some money. And since she didn't see how she was ever going to make any money with Sallie Martin, she left. By the time her mother had summoned the proper amount of righteous indignation, Dinah had also married John Young and left home.

The story goes that Mrs. Jones, furious with her daughter for leaving Sallie Martin and the world of gospel music, and certain that Dinah was selling her soul to the devil, insisted that John Young accompany Dinah to and from the South Side bars where she got singing jobs. This order, if indeed it was ever given, presented no hardship for Young, who was acting as Dinah's agent at the time.

John Young got Dinah her first jobs singing in South Side clubs, and during her first year out of gospel she played at a variety of night spots. She spent three weeks at Dave's Café, later called the Rhumboogie, and was sufficiently well

received there to get an invitation to help open the new
Down Beat Room of the Sherman Hotel, whose first show
starred Fats Waller. Waller was impressed with her singing
and during his four weeks there touted her widely. Later he
claimed to have discovered her, but other than talking her
up during his four-week engagement at the Down Beat Room,
he did little to further her "career"—which only a starry-
eyed youngster with visions of Billie Holiday dancing in
her head could call the string of jobs Dinah was getting.
Most of the South Side clubs were small, their clientele
working-class or two-bit sporting-life types with more blus-
ter than bankroll. Dinah rarely received a salary and had to
rely on tips or a percentage of the nightly take. Perhaps
John Young had envisioned something bigger quicker for
his wife, or perhaps he objected to the seediness of the
South Side club world; then, too, Ruth may have been too
friendly with other men in the clubs. Whatever Young's
reasons, according to Dinah he changed his mind about her
career and objected to her working in the clubs. She refused
to listen. "We stayed together three months," she later said,
"then he went into the army. I knew we were through, and
I guess he did too."

Dinah was playing piano at the Three Deuces, yet another South Side jazz club, when a friend named Martha
Davis took her to hear Billie Holiday at the Garrick Stage
Lounge. Although Holiday was a major star in the black
community by that time, legend has it that Joe Sherman,
manager of the bar and a man not known for his ency-
clopedic knowledge of jazz, had booked her thinking she
was a man. But working with a sextet led by trumpeter Red
Allen, Billie was drawing them in, and Sherman knew enough
not to argue with the sound of a busy cash register. Dinah
was not surprised that Billie was drawing the people in;
Billie was still her idol, and Dinah would still do whatever
was necessary to hear her, or even see her. She was not

disappointed by Billie's performance at the Garrick Stage Lounge—in fact, she was mesmerized and returned night after night. Learning that Lady Day would be in residence at the downstairs rooms of the Garrick for three months, Dinah determined to get a job in the upstairs room in order to be near her.

At the time, the Cats and the Fiddle band were holding forth upstairs. Dinah informed Joe Sherman that he needed a singer, and he agreed to audition her. Backed by the Cats and the Fiddle, she sang "I Understand" and impressed Sherman enough to get the job. Thereafter, Dinah would finish her set and then rush downstairs to listen to and watch Lady Day, making mental notes on her stage demeanor as well as her phrasing. In fact, Joe Sherman complained that she was never where she ought to be. Lady Day sang without extravagant gestures: She swayed her body slightly, snapped her fingers to the tempo, relied on her voice to hold the attention of the audience. Dinah was accustomed to more outright acting on stage and she began to tone down her own presentation, trying to see if she, too, could hold an audience with the sheer power of her singing. She studied Holiday's singing style closely, too. According to Jimmy Cobb, to whom she later spoke often of her time playing at Garrick's upstairs from Billie Holiday, "She got so she could mimic Lady Day—she could really sound like her. Later, every now and then she would do that on the stage —not too often, but when something led up to it, and she felt good, she would do it." Trouble was, when the three months were up, Lady Day moved on. She ended the year with a hugely successful booking at the Regal Theater with Lionel Hampton's band where, on New Year's Eve, according to *Down Beat*, they "tore the roof off." Dinah remained at Garrick's Stage Lounge, making fifty dollars a week and impressing Joe Sherman enough to cause him to try to help further her career by inviting her downstairs to sing whenever he thought there was someone in the audience who could help her. He is also generally credited with having suggested that she change her name to Dinah Washington. According to one account, he was discussing billing with his new singer and pointed out that her name was "too dry, too commonplace. You ought to have a name that rolls off people's tongues like rich liquor." No doubt Ruth Jones liked that image. Sherman doodled for a while on a blotter, then slapped the table in front of him and shouted, "I've got it! Let's change your name to Dinah . . . Dinah . . . Washington." Others claim to have given her that name, including Joe Glaser and Lionel Hampton.

Joe Glaser stopped by the club one night in 1943, on the invitation of Joe Sherman, according to some stories. He was a veteran at discovering and booking black talent, having operated the Sunset Café in Chicago with Ed Fox, and having headed the Rockwell–O'Keefe Agency's colored-band department for some years and counting among his clients Louis Armstrong, Hot Lips Page, Willie Bryant, Andy Kirk, and Claude Hopkins, not to mention Lionel Hampton, whose band he had booked into the Regal Theater in Chicago for a month's engagement. He heard Dinah sing and he knew he had found in her special blend of pop, gospel, and jazz a talent to be reckoned with. Not long afterward, he brought Lionel Hampton to Garrick's to hear her.

Hampton, whose big band was then about five and a half years old, had been nurtured in the big-band style by none other than Benny Goodman, the King of Swing, who was the first white bandleader to defy the unwritten laws that segregated white and black jazz musicians when he invited black pianist Teddy Wilson to join his group. Arriving in Los Angeles in 1936, Goodman and some of his men had gone to the Paradise Club and been impressed by Hampton's versatility—Hamp was playing drums, vibes, and piano as the occasion warranted. Hampton recorded with Goodman almost immediately and accepted Goodman's invitation to join his band provided that his girlfriend, Gladys Neal, could accompany him. Gladys's mother refused to allow her daughter to travel with Hampton unless they were married, so on their way to New York to join Goodman they tied the knot. Gladys had exceptional business acumen, and while traveling with the Goodman band she learned all she could about the band business; within a year she had learned enough to urge her husband to go out on his own.

The first Hampton bands were packed with talent, even though performers received only ten dollars a performance —money that they had to make last all week if they did not play more than one night. Gladys paid for their uniforms and for their professional dry-cleaning bills, as well as providing transportation, but the band members were responsible for their own lodging and food costs. Irving Ashby, who was a member of the Hampton band from 1940 to 1941, recalls that after a year his salary was raised to eleven dollars a performance. By 1942, according to Marshall Royal, who was with the band from 1940 to 1942, the men were getting fourteen dollars a performance.

Working conditions were as poor as the salaries in those early years. The band wasn't well known and was forced to accept one-night engagements in small towns all over. But all the while the band was recording, and by late 1942 to early 1943, the Lionel Hampton Orchestra had a substantial following, both for live performances and for its records. Hampton himself also had a sizable capital base, thanks to Gladys and to Joe Glaser. "We were hired cheap, and sold for a lot of money," recalls Marshall Royal. "I once overheard Joe Glaser telling Gladys backstage, 'When you get these guys, you've got to hire them as cheap as you can and sell them for as much as you can.' That's when I quit."

In late 1942, when the orchestra arrived in Chicago,

Hampton, in his recollection, did not have a girl singer. Comedian Slappy White, who was traveling at the time with the Hampton band as half of an act called the Two Zephyrs, has a different recollection—he remembers that Hampton had a couple of them: "Hampton had a girl named Madeline Green with him, and Madeline Green came from Earl Hines's band—Hines had both her and Billy Eckstine. Hamp also had Ruby Blakely." Jimmy Cobb also believes that Hampton had at least one girl singer at the time. Apparently, however, they were not singers-in-residence with Hampton. According to Leonard Feather, both Joe Williams and Ruby Blakely were with Hampton on a part-time basis. Perhaps because he continued to record only instrumentals and most of the singers wanted to record, he could not keep any of them for long. But girl singers had become almost a requirement for big bands in live performance, and Joe Glaser, at least, believed that Hampton should hear the girl at Garrick's. Slappy White recalls that in addition to Glaser, some other members of the Hampton band, among them Snooky Young and Clark Terry, were in the bar that night and when they heard Dinah sing "Sweet Georgia Brown," they were as impressed with her voice as Glaser was. Whoever told Lionel Hampton about the girl, he was interested enough to take himself to the bar that night as well.

In Hampton's recollection, Dinah was not singing at Garrick's when he first heard her; she was working as an attendant in the ladies' washroom. That image of Ruth Jones as a hapless washroom attendant has gained a firm foothold in Dinah Washington legend, but it is not true. Perhaps Hampton judged her station by her clothes, which were pretty "raggedy," according to those who knew her at the time. Hampton remembers his first impression of the girl as she emerged from the basement: "She was an innocent-looking coloured girl with a chest that revealed that she could really belt it out. Without saying hello or asking who

I was, she began singing 'Sweet Georgia Brown.' As she later told me, she was only ushered to the main floor in order to sing. So there was no need to ask questions. After having listened to a few bars, I knew that she was the girl I was looking for. She could make herself heard, even with my blazing band in the background. And she had that blues quality that would contrast beautifully with my swinging style. 'What's your name?' I asked. 'Ruth Jones.' 'You can't become a star with that name. We'll find you another one,' I hinted. 'I don't care how you call me, as long as you let me sing,' she answered and, after a pause, added, 'And as long as you pay me.' ''

Hampton continues, ''I recalled at that moment that as a child I had asked my grandmother, 'Do ladies' rooms smell the same way men's rooms do?' She had thought it over for a while, then decided it was an obscene question and had quenched my curiosity with a good spanking. Ever since, I had felt prejudiced against public rest rooms, and I was therefore especially proud to be able to liberate this young woman from toiling in the toilets.''

The following afternoon Dinah joined Hampton's band at the Regal Theater for a quick rehearsal. The Regal was Chicago's answer to the Palace in New York—it had a huge stage and a resident company, including the Regalettes dancers—but neither the opportunity to perform at a big-time theater nor the chance to join a reigning big band like Lionel Hampton's fazed the young Dinah. Slappy White recalls that she was remarkably composed: ''Hamp said, 'Ladies and gentlemen, here's Ruth Jones, Chicago girl Ruth Jones,' and she walked out there and sang and she stopped that show cold.''

As mentioned above, Lionel Hampton also takes credit for giving Ruth Jones the name Dinah Washington. He does not recall why that name came to him, ''but that's the way it was.'' And when the Hampton band's engagement at the

Regal Theater ended, there was no question in Hampton's mind that Dinah Washington would accompany the group to their next engagement in Detroit. "The next date was the Paradise Theater in Detroit," says Slappy White, "and he blended her right into the show. And then he had to put her down next to closing because she was so strong—yeah, she stopped that show, she stopped every show cold." Lionel Hampton took her on. Said Dinah to Leonard Feather of *Down Beat* in 1952, "A few weeks later I bought two traveling bags, on time—some friends signed for me; I was getting $50 a week at the Garrick."

On the road, and making seventy-five dollars a week, Dinah continued to stop the Hampton shows cold, but the word can be applied to opposite feelings, and unfortunately for Dinah, offstage she also turned the members of Lionel Hampton's band cold. They allowed as to how she had great talent, but they didn't think much of her looks. Offstage, Dinah's confidence evaporated. "At that time, it was like a thing about being dark," says Jimmy Cobb, referring to the standard image of light-complected Negro beauty. Dorothy Dandridge and Lena Horne in Hollywood, Billie Holiday on big-band podiums—these were the ideals. Hampton's other girl singers were light-skinned and well dressed and very attractive. Dinah, although she'd gotten over the adolescent skin problem that had given rise to the nickname Alligator, was not a looker. About five foot seven she was plump and top heavy, and her facial features, from eyes to nose to mouth, were over-large and overpowering. "Dinah," says Cobb, "didn't have nuthin'—she was raggedy—and so she went through that kind of number, and I think it kind of stuck to her a little bit." George Dixon, who played with Earl Hines, remembered the reaction of the Hampton band to Dinah clearly enough to tell Stanley Dance, author of *The World of Earl Hines,* about it some thirty-five years later: "They'd just heard Ol' Hamp had got a new singer. They thought a great, big, beautiful girl was going to walk out, and when they saw Dinah Washington everybody covered their head up. Except Slappy White. He talked to her, and was nice to her, and it paid off for him.''

Slappy White and his partner had been alternating between Louis Armstrong's and Lionel Hampton's bands, because Joe Glaser acted as agent for a number of bands, as well as for the Two Zephyrs. By the time Dinah joined Hampton, however, Hampton was ''getting hot,'' as White puts it, and White performed almost exclusively with Hampton: ''See, at that time, we used to travel in buses and when Dinah went on tour with us—you know, Dinah was just an average girl—we'd get into a town like Youngstown, Ohio, or Akron or somewhere that we were playing those one-day theaters, two-day theaters. When the bus pulled into town, all the boys would jump off and run to their rooms. We'd get rooms in people's houses in those days. They'd run off and get their rooms, and poor Dinah didn't know what to do. I came back on the bus one day to get something and she was sitting on the bus crying because she didn't have no room and all the band was gone. So I said, 'Well, come on, you can have my room.' So I gave her my room and went and found me another room and from then on we got to be buddies. She wasn't the best-looking girl in the world so the band boys . . . wasn't nobody hitting on her, you know? They were looking for the girl around the stage door. So she kind of warmed up to me, and then when she got big, she never forgot.''

Although she would not forget the callous way the members of the band treated her, Dinah did not complain. Instead, she developed a tough, one-of-the-boys manner of dealing with them—joking with them, playing the card game Tonk with them, cursing like the proverbial sailor. According to Slappy White, she also patterned her love life after theirs. ''The musicians, every town we'd go in, they'd have a different girl. The bus would pull up, and the girls would be waiting, and they'd hang around the stage door and backstage. Now Dinah Washington, she's with the band, too, so she required the same things that the band did. It's all right for musicians to do it, but if a girl does it, why is it wrong?'' Like Snooky Young, Dexter Gordon, Shadow Wilson, Clark Terry, and the others, she adopted an attitude of exaggerated interest in the opposite sex, making a game of bold suggestions and overabundant compliments. After a while, Dinah was accepted by the other band members. They liked her, and once they liked her, she became more attractive to them. Jack Wilson, a piano player who joined Dinah in 1958, recalls, ''When we were in Detroit, Lucky Thompson, the great tenor-saxophone star who was with the Hampton band when Dinah was there, came to visit her. He told me that Dinah always had pretty legs and that the guys in the [Hampton] band used to call her Legs. We started noticing after that—Dinah did have beautiful legs.''

By the time Dinah joined the Hampton band, the lean days, when the entire group sometimes subsisted on rice and ketchup, were over. The seventy-five dollars a week that Hampton was paying her she considered big money compared with what she had made before. But lodging was as big a problem as ever. There was hardly a white hotel in the country that would admit blacks, and there were few black hotels. Slappy White remembers, ''The Gotham Hotel in Detroit was the first big-time black hotel in show business. Everybody wanted to play Detroit, because when you got to Detroit, you were going to live at the Gotham.'' In most cities, there were black boardinghouses, but the best that some black communities could offer were private homes. Recalls Marshall Royal, ''When you'd work in the South, you'd come into a town at three o'clock in the morning on a bus and everybody would get out of the bus and start

going from house to house and door to door ringing door-
bells and asking people could we stay in their house? Did
they have an extra room to rent? There were homes that
were known for renting rooms. They had people who would
give you a room and also cook meals for you. That was so
in the North, too. You'd come in and rent a room in the
morning and you'd leave your stuff in the room and go to
work. During the course of the night the people that owned
the house would come in and take your bags out of your
room and rent it to a couple that wanted to come there to
turn a trick that night. You'd come back, and your bags
would be in the hallway, and liable to be somebody still in
your room. That's the way we lived. Meals were a problem,
too—you were lucky if you got one good meal a day,
because you couldn't get served in most restaurants. And
that wasn't only in the South. Portland, Oregon, was the
one city where I remember I couldn't even get a hot dog.''

Dinah didn't mind all that. She drew sustenance from
the audiences, who consistently gave her standing ovations
in the cities and towns to which she traveled with the Hampton band. Gladys Hampton also took pity on her and began
to give her "little things, like shoes and stuff," according
to Jimmy Cobb. "When Gladys found out she could sing
as good as she could, she started to try to make her look
better.'' Gladys Hampton loved shoes, and when she noticed
that Dinah had pretty feet, she encouraged her to show them
off. "Gladys used to be the seamstress for some movie
star—Norma Shearer or somebody,'' says Slappy White.
"Gladys had a hell of a taste in clothes. Gladys would tell
Dinah what to wear and had Dinah looking good. Dinah
would see the type of stuff that Gladys would wear, but
Dinah couldn't afford to wear the shoes that Gladys Hampton was wearing, because Gladys was spending $150 to
$200 at a time for shoes. But she would give Dinah some
of her old shoes, and they were still good.'' Hampton him-

self treated her with respect, and her one, unvoiced criticism was that he continued to pursue his traditional formula of recording only instrumentals, finding no room in that formula for a girl singer, no matter how beautiful or strong her voice. Dinah was no fool; she knew that the key to fame was records, and she wanted to make them.

Records were becoming major consumer items. While in the entire decade of the 1930s only twenty-six records each sold a million copies, in the first half of the 1940s sixty-eight records sold a million copies or more, and this despite serious shortages of materials due to the war. But since Hampton's recording success was with instrumentals, Dinah resigned herself to the fact that as long as she was with Hampton, she would not get the opportunity to record.

With Hampton, Dinah made her debut at the Apollo Theater, famous for having the toughest audiences in the world. If they didn't like you at the Apollo, you were liable to get rotten tomatoes thrown in your face; but if they loved you, you'd cracked the toughest nut in black show business. Though the Apollo was owned by the white Schiffman family, it catered to the surrounding black community and featured the biggest black names in the entertainment world. Because of its star acts, it also attracted a substantial number of white lovers of black musical sounds, among them Leonard Feather—and much later, a very young Elvis Presley. Hampton and his band had first delighted the Apollo audiences in 1940, and so by 1943, when Dinah went into the theater with the Hampton band, she faced a crowd that was standing-room-only and eager to like her. She made them like her for herself.

In December 1943, the Hampton band arrived in New York to play the lucrative holiday season. It was then that Leonard Feather heard Dinah for the first time. The young songwriter and agent remembers her as "a chubby youngster, brash and confident" whose singing impressed him greatly. "I knew Lionel quite well, so I went backstage and met her," Feather recalls. "I don't remember what she was singing at the time, but she wasn't singing blues, and I thought she'd make a wonderful blues singer. I was doing quite a bit of blues writing at the time, and I got the idea of writing some blues songs for her and taking a few guys out of the band and recording her. Lionel's band was very, very popular as an instrumental orchestra, so he was recording nothing but instrumentals, he wasn't recording vocals."

Feather even had a recording company in mind. Keynote Records was an independent company founded by Eric Bernay and regarded by some as the first independent record company. Bernay also had a legendary record store on West Forty-fourth Street in Manhattan called the Music Room, right next door to an avant-garde bookstore called Book Fair, and the two stores influenced a generation of young intellectuals. According to Leonard Feather, Bernay started Keynote as a classical-music recording company. Arnold Shaw believes his first recordings were of jazz. At any rate, Bernay was at that time branching out. In November 1942 the company issued a gospel record, "Praise the Lord," by the Royal Harmony Quartet, which did well, and Bernay started to dream of giving bigger labels, such as Capitol, Bluebird, Victor, and Decca, a run for their money in the race-record market. Feather approached Bernay with the idea of recording some blues sides with the young Dinah Washington and some members of Lionel Hampton's band, and Bernay agreed.

"Joe Morris was the trumpet player," recalls Feather, "and Rudy Rutherford was on clarinet, Arnett Cobb on tenor saxophone, Milt Buckner on piano, Vernon King on bass, and Fred Radcliffe on the drums. After they got through at the Apollo Theater—it must have been eleven o'clock or midnight—we went to this little RKO studio in Radio

City Center on the twenty-ninth of December 1943 and made four tunes. Only one of them, 'Homeward Bound,' was especially written for Dinah. The others had been written in 1940 and recorded by other artists, but nothing had happened. One was a rewrite of a tune that I had written originally for a man, and I rewrote the lyrics for Dinah. It was 'Evil Gal Blues.' That was the most famous one; it was the biggest hit of the four. Another one was 'Salty Papa Blues,' which also became very well known and which Dinah eventually recorded again many years later. There was also one called 'I Know How to Do It.' ''

Each was recorded with great professionalism and in a minimum amount of time by the young but self-possessed Dinah. ''She wasn't nervous at all,'' says Feather, ''she just went straight ahead. She learned the lyrics up front, of course, and she just took to it like a duck takes to water.'' She enjoyed working with the seasoned sidemen, whom Bernay and Feather dubbed the Lionel Hampton Sextet, and the musicians enjoyed working with her. No one realized that the recording session was contractually illegal. At the time, Lionel Hampton was under contract with Decca, the leading jazz recording company, but neither Feather nor Eric Bernay nor the members of the Hampton band who became the Lionel Hampton Sextet saw any conflict. Even Hampton went along with it. ''Lionel knew about the session. It wasn't done behind his back or anything,'' says Feather. ''In fact, in the middle of the session he came in and said hello to everybody and gladhanded us all and sat in voluntarily. He played drums on 'I Know How to Do It' and piano—that two-finger style of his—on 'Homeward Bound.' I said, 'You sure this is okay, Lionel?' and he said, 'Oh yeah, no, don't worry about it.' ''

Actually, Hampton played on all four sides that were recorded during that session. He also played vibes on ''Evil Gal Blues'' and ''Salty Papa Blues.'' Listening to those

recordings, one can easily understand why Hampton would
have wanted to be a part of them, for it is evident in all
four sides that the musicians were having a great time—
including the musician Dinah Washington, whose high, clear
voice was like a tenor sax at times, like a clarinet at others.
"She had a very biting tone quality to her voice, a unique
timbre. Nobody else had quite that sound," says Leonard
Feather. "She had a style that reflected her church and
gospel background and the whole tradition of the blues. She
didn't sound like Bessie Smith, but it was in the same
tradition, just a generation later—a more sophisticated sound,
with a more sophisticated background accompanying music." Her easy relationship with the musicians was remi-
niscent of Billie Holiday, whose influence is evident in at
least one of the sides, "Salty Papa Blues." Each side includes substantial solos by her accompanists—pianist Milt
Buckner and trumpeter Joe Morris on "Evil Gal Blues,"
tenor-sax man Arnett Cobb on "I Know How to Do It,"
Morris and Cobb on "Salty Papa Blues," and clarinetist
Rudy Rutherford and both Hampton and Buckner at the
piano on "Homeward Bound." Clearly, a good time was
had by all, making music for themselves, jamming rather
than performing, until 4:30 A.M.

Gladys Hampton felt differently. She handled the business, and Hampton has often said she had the head for
business that he never had. If she'd known beforehand about
the recording session with Dinah Washington and the Lionel
Hampton Sextet, she would never have allowed it. She knew
that Lionel's contract with Decca did not permit moonlight-
ing by members of his band, particularly not when they
called themselves the Lionel Hampton Sextet.

"All hell broke loose," recalls Leonard Feather, "because the records were immediate hits and they had Lionel's
name on them. Gladys was furious. There was a big story
about it in *Billboard* magazine. Keynote had to change the

labels and take Lionel's name off them and call the group
Sextet with Dinah Washington. But, anyhow, the records
were very, very successful, particularly 'Evil Gal Blues'
and 'Salty Papa.' They were my first real hits as a composer.
And Dinah Washington suddenly became a name instead
of just a vocalist for the orchestra.''

She became ''a name'' in a relatively unsung but quite
lucrative market called the race market. Only the most die-
hard aficionados of black music heard these records, which
were sold in black neighborhoods—often in the back rooms
of ghetto businesses and sometimes even from the tailgates
of cars—for play primarily on jukeboxes. Although home
record players were becoming increasingly popular, most
people did not yet own one, and *Billboard* magazine would
not introduce its ''Honor Roll of Hits'' (its first pop chart)
until 1945. Certainly, the majority of the black population
did not own record players. So, when it is said that Dinah
Washington's first solo recordings were hits, the reference
is to a very small, and primarily black, market—a market
that consisted chiefly of black clubs that could afford to
have jukeboxes. Still, it was a market that the record companies, major and minor, had their eyes on, and Dinah's
success did not go unremarked.

Decca, and Lionel Hampton, however, felt no urge to
capitalize on Dinah's success. According to Dinah, Hampton kept promising her that she could record, but nothing
came of it. Leonard Feather quotes her as saying, ''One
day I got up very early to rush over to a session; Hamp had
promised to let me record 'Million Dollar Smile.' But some-
how it wound up being a vibes solo. I still don't know
whether Decca or Lionel was to blame.''

Not yet twenty-one years old, Dinah Washington was a
strong presence on the black-music charts and a talent, at
least on stage, to be reckoned with in the Hampton organization. Hampton now featured her in his concerts and on

occasion allowed her to sing the blues songs at which she was so good, though her segments of each show were never allowed to overshadow the overall big-band emphasis. Throughout 1944, at the Strand, Apollo, and Capital theaters in New York, at Symphony Hall in Boston, at the State Theater in Hartford, and at all the theaters in between, Dinah was Lionel Hampton's girl singer. She was not by any means the star, although under different circumstances she could have been.

She was not ready to go out on her own, however. For all the considerable life experience that her wide eyes seemed to belie, she was young and not very sure of herself. In spite of all the drawbacks, she felt comfortable in the Hampton organization. She maintained a fairly good relationship with Gladys Hampton (though Gladys now expected to be paid for the cast-off clothes she gave Dinah) and studied the way Gladys did business as closely as she had once studied the singing and stage gestures of Billie Holiday. Gladys was a woman who knew how to function in the predominantly man's world of show business, and Dinah admired her for it.

She was also learning a great deal about music. Much of it was big-band music, but it was music nevertheless. If she did not fit the physical image of the standard big-band singer of the time—she couldn't get by with the flared skirts and prim collars and short white gloves favored by a singer like Anita O'Day—she was, like O'Day, steeping herself in the sounds of the instruments and learning to make an instrument of her voice. The emotions, however, were all her own. She had the capacity, and communicated it to her audiences, of having much more to express than she was allowed, of being like a volcano that threatened always to explode. The material she was given to sing she imbued with as much emotion as she could, cognizant always of her position in the organization and aware that it was not in her best interests ever to try to "steal the show." In the meantime, she was aware that with Hampton she was getting the kind of exposure that she would not have been able to get as easily if she were on her own.

Finally, on May 21, 1945, Dinah went into the Decca recording studios with an all-star sextet culled from Hampton's regular group for a contractually legal session. One of the songs she recorded was a Leonard Feather composition called "Blowtop Blues." "I more or less wrote that for her—it was very much in character for her," Feather recalls, "and she made it sound very convincing. Some of the lines were, 'Last night I was five feet tall, today I'm eight feet ten. Every time I fall down, I float right up again.' She sang the hell out of that."

In the same month as Dinah recorded "Blowtop Blues," the Hampton Orchestra performed at Carnegie Hall in a concert staged by Feather. "When Dinah sang 'Evil Gal Blues,' Lionel had me come on and take over for Milt Buckner and play piano for her on just that one number," says Feather. Dinah was also featured on a large concert album of Hampton's issued by Decca. But, according to Feather, "Lionel [was] unhappy with us because he couldn't get the publishing rights [to "Blowtop Blues"], and feuding with Dinah about other matters. [He] didn't let the record out until many months later, after she had worked her way up to $125 a week and finally quit the band." According to Dinah legend, she had to use a gun to persuade Hampton to release both the record and her from her contract.

It was a combination of money considerations and artistic considerations that caused Dinah to decide to leave Lionel Hampton's band. Hampton was not paying her what she now considered she was worth, and she often felt stifled singing big-band songs. Although she was known to brag that she could sing anything at all, she realized after her records for Keynote did so well that her blues songs were best received, and with Hampton she did not get much opportunity to sing the blues. Nor did she do any further recording with Hampton—in the two-plus years she was with him, "Blowtop Blues" was the only officially sanctioned song on which she was featured. Explains Leonard Feather, "Decca figured, who needs a singer with Lionel Hampton's band? They just wanted to record him playing the vibraphone." Dinah saw that if she wanted a chance to record and sing more blues, she would have to leave Hampton and go out on her own.

It was not as big a step for a twenty-two-year-old as it appeared. She already had a name of sorts, thanks to the blues songs she had recorded and to the publicity attendant on Decca's threatened lawsuit because of those recordings. According to Leonard Feather, she was already recognized as "probably the most important new R&B recording star of the decade." Dinah had learned a lot during her time with Hampton. Playing gigs across the country, she had met hundreds of musicians and felt as if she belonged to that far-flung family—no matter where she went, she knew she would find someone she knew. By the time she left Hampton, she had become involved with George Jenkins, a drummer who had played with both Hampton's and Budd Johnson's orchestras, and he encouraged her to go out on her own. Joe Glaser was eager to book her. And—she had been offered the chance to record with Apollo Records.

On Her Own

APOLLO Records, an independent company that had no relationship to the Apollo Theater, had grown out of a Harlem record store in the early 1940s and involved three partners—Hy Seigal, Sam Schneider, and Ike Berman. During the war, the three men had talked of forming their own record label, but wartime shortages of materials such as shellac precluded their acting on their dreams. The production of new records had been cut drastically. Even big companies had to scavenge old disks, which were melted down and rerolled for new pressing. Independent companies barely stayed alive, and not a few folded. When the war ended, however, the record business began to open up again. Postwar prosperity brought demand for records, and for a smart, would-be independent company the time was right. Siegal, Schneider, and Berman formed Apollo.

Ike's wife, Bess, did not have her name on any of the formal agreements, but she soon became the moving force behind the company. It was she who led it into both blues and gospel, fields that were comparatively neglected by the big companies. Within the space of a few months, she signed both Dinah Washington and Mahalia Jackson, whose eight-year association with the company would bring fame not only to herself but to Apollo. Coincidentally, both Mahalia Jackson and Dinah Washington had enjoyed the tutelage of the great gospel singer Sallie Martin. Not coincidentally, the two avenues into which Bess Berman directed Apollo were intimately related. Blues was secularized gospel; while Mahalia Jackson lifted her listeners to the heights of religious ecstasy, Dinah Washington ushered them into gardens of more earthly delights.

It was for the purpose of recording for Apollo that Dinah made her first trip to the West Coast, where in December 1945 she entered a Los Angeles recording studio three times—the tenth, the twelfth, and the thirteenth—to make twelve sides for four labels: Apollo, ABC, Grand Award, and Parrot, each of which had different geographical markets and each of which, as independents, had found that it was economically advantageous to share production costs. It was also economically advantageous for Apollo not to pay its recording artists much money—Dinah got an advance of $1,800. She was backed by Lucky Thompson and his All Stars, which included Thompson on tenor sax, Lee Young on guitar, Charles Mingus on bass, Milt Jackson on vibraharp, Wilbert Baranco on piano, and Eugene Porter on baritone sax. Except for two novelty tunes called "No Voot—No Boot" and "My Voot Is Really Vout," the sides were all blues numbers: "Wise Woman Blues," "My Lovin' Papa," "Mellow Mama Blues," "Walking Woman Blues," "Rich Man's Blues," "Beggin' Woman Blues," "All or Nothing," "Blues for a Day," "Chewin' Woman Blues." All the blues numbers featured Dinah's ballad style at its best, a sound that breathed sensuality. The descriptive words used by critics are instructive: *velvet, silken*. Writes Arnold Shaw, "in its bluer moments, it tore like silk, not satin."

Dinah's mother, Alice Jones, did not like to hear such descriptions, but she had mellowed in her attitude toward Dinah's secular career. According to Jimmy Cobb, who knew the family well in the early fifties, "When she went out with Lionel Hampton and got to be a little sort of light hit, her mother liked it." Dinah sent as much as she could from her salary and record earnings back home and promised her mother that she would soon buy her a house. Mrs. Jones decided that singing music other than gospel might not be so bad after all.

The wax on Dinah's recordings for Apollo et al. was barely dry when Dinah got a chance to record for Mercury, a fledging label that had been founded in late 1945 in Chicago. An agent named Ben Bart approached Dinah with a package deal. He would get her a recording contract with Mercury Records, which would take over distribution of her recordings for Apollo, and act as her manager-booker at the same time. Dinah immediately accepted, terminated her arrangement with Joe Glaser, and within a month she was back in Chicago, recording her first sides for Mercury, with which label she would stay for more than fifteen years.

She was backed by trombonist Gus Chappell and his orchestra on these sides. According to trumpeter Sonny Cohn, Pee Wee Jackson was on trumpet for that session. The songs they recorded were not blues songs. Instead, they were pop songs and "covers" for popular songs recorded by white singers that in the segregated music business of the time could not be issued in the Negro market unless they were sung by a black singer. "Embraceable You," "I Can't Get Started," "When a Woman Loves a Man," and "Joy Juice," may have expressed universal sentiments, but the recordings could not be universally distributed. Dinah Washington became Mercury's resident "cover girl."

During that session, Dinah and Chappell had a brief relationship, inspired in part by the fact that they had gone to the same high school in Chicago and also by their mutual love of music and dreams of making it in the music world. But Dinah was traveling a lot, and it was the men whom she saw most regularly who benefited from her attention. Slappy White was among them, and though the two were never more than buddies, they were practically inseparable, given their respective schedules.

A star of the race-record charts was in no position to sit at home resting on her laurels. Dinah had to get out and work. And the young Mercury record company could not record her unless she happened to be in a city where there were suitable facilities. That meant that Dinah did a lot of one-night and two-night stands in many places between recording dates and that when she happened to be in New York or Chicago or Los Angeles playing a date, she also recorded. Personal appearances, not recordings, were her bread and butter, and as such she was no different from most black musicmakers of the time. They made their living traveling from city to city, and town to town, playing one-night stands and glad for the work, staying in private homes and, when they could, two-bit hotels.

It was in one such hotel that Gordon Austin first met Dinah. Austin, a trombonist out of Pittsburgh, had played with Fletcher Henderson originally and in 1946 was with Earl "Fatha" Hines's Orchestra, along with Lucky Millinder, who produced the shows, and drummer George Jenkins. "We met in the Braddock Hotel in New York, on the way to the bathroom," Austin recalls. "They didn't have rooms with private baths at the Braddock. In fact, in those days, if you could find a room with a bath, you were lucky. I was going to the bathroom to take a shower, and I had on a short robe, and she came passing by and said, 'Ummm, boy you sure got some pretty legs.' From then on, she called me Pretty Legs. I don't know why she took up with me. All these people ran across Dinah, but she just took up with certain people. Like I said, I don't know why she took up with me."

Gordon Austin was not one of Dinah's lovers, although

at the time they met, they might have been. Austin's first marriage had broken up not long after he had left Pittsburgh with Fletcher Henderson's band. Dinah had been divorced from John Young for some three years. But they were close friends only—at least as close as musicians on the road could be. Although both traveled a lot—Austin with the Hines band, and Dinah with her musicians—they often found themselves in the same town. "We'd meet in Saint Louis," says Austin, "and it was, 'Where you gonna be tomorrow night?' We'd compare our itineraries and say, 'Well, I'll see you in Detroit.' That's all we did, just traveled, day in and day out. Before the war we mostly traveled on buses, but then the war broke out and they took the buses from us because they needed them for the troops, so we had to drive cars. You couldn't get too many people to drive cars, because it was hard and you couldn't get any rest; but some of the guys would drive for extra pay. Then they started rationing gas, and that cut down on our schedule for a while, but they would try to get us as close to the next date as possible. We concentrated on the major cities, where we could stay a week or two. But mostly it was one-nighters, especially for black musicians."

And for black musicians, those one-nighters were often in small places that didn't pay much. The places where Dinah played were frequently what Austin calls "nitty-gritty places"—tobacco barns and honky-tonks. The size of her band varied accordingly. When Austin met her in New York, she was traveling with a ten-piece band. Most of the time, however, "she dropped down to six pieces. She'd go into a club with three horns and three rhythms, and in some places she'd have only two horns, and sometimes she'd only have the rhythm section. It all depended on the size of the club and what she could get out of it moneywise." Accordingly, the personnel roster of her traveling band was very fluid, with musicians checking in and checking out with great regularity. They could not hang around waiting for Dinah to get a well-paying gig in a sizable club, and she did not expect them to. And what disadvantages accrued to that situation for her logistically were, in retrospect, more than outweighed by the advantages of working with a great number of very fine musicians. When Dinah reached the level at which she was able to choose the musicians with whom she would record, she had very definite ideas about whom she wanted at each session.

Gordon Austin never actually accompanied her. When they found themselves together, he usually did errands. "I used to go to the store for her and all. I was like her brother. I never felt as if she was using me. In fact, she would say, 'Sometimes I feel I'm taking advantage of you.' I'd say, 'If I didn't want to do it, I wouldn't do it. Please believe me.' She'd say, 'That's why I love you. You're like my big brother.' " There were not a lot of other people in her life like Gordon Austin; most of the people around her wanted something.

According to Austin, that included George Jenkins, who had left the Hines band to become featured drummer with the Budd Johnson Orchestra and whose path often crossed Dinah's during the spring and early summer of 1946. In April, the Johnson Orchestra was in Los Angeles when Dinah was there to record "Oo-Wee-Walkie Talkie" with Gerald Wilson's Orchestra (Snooky Young on trumpet). She and Jenkins, who'd been a drummer with Lionel Hampton when Dinah had joined the Hampton Orchestra, had been eyeing each other for years. Still, it came as a surprise to many of her friends, among them Gordon Austin, when in July 1946 she and Jenkins were married. "That never did look right to some of the guys, including myself—her relationship with George and getting married and all. They were two opposite people. It all happened so fast, I don't think anybody realized what was going on. I don't know how that wedding happened. All I knew was, when we came back to Chicago, they were married.''

Dinah was soon pregnant and forced to confront her ideas about what she wanted to be: She longed for the one thing she felt she had been deprived of as a child, a stable family. Though only in her early twenties, she'd already seen enough of life to have decided that she wanted a home base and a family she could count on, and in her youthful enthusiasm did not think about the fact that there might be others instrumental in that stability, among them her husband. Unfortunately, she also had to pay the bills, for her husband was a spender, not a saver—''As soon as we had a bankroll, he'd blow it,'' she said later—so she took whatever bookings and recording dates Ben Bart could get for her.

While George Jenkins was on the road with Charlie Barnett's band, Ben Bart arranged bookings for Dinah in Los Angeles and New York and a lot of small cities and towns in between during the latter part of 1946. In New York, she finally had a chance to record blues for Mercury, recording ''A Slick Chick,'' ''Postman Blues,'' and ''That's When a Woman Loves a Heel'' with Tab Smith's Orchestra; but she also did more covers backed by Chubby Jackson's Orchestra, among them ''Stairway to the Stars'' and ''I Want to Be Loved.''

As her pregnancy progressed, she spent more time in Chicago. ''She was working in clubs in and around Chicago, trying to do what she could to make things work,'' says Gordon Austin. ''Meanwhile, George was traveling with the band. He was a great drummer, but he wanted to play around and all that. And she wanted to be a housewife, though she wanted her career, too. She wanted that feeling that when they got done work, they could go to their home and be together. But it didn't work out that way, and after about six or seven months the relationship started to get stormy.''

''While I was pregnant, I heard from him but sparingly,

and he'd send money home when he felt like it," Dinah told Dave Hepburn for an article titled "Me and My Six Husbands." "I made up my mind that as soon as I got back on my feet, that would be the end."

Toward the end of her pregnancy, and after she gave birth to George Jenkins, Jr., in 1947, Dinah was unable to make personal appearances. Drummer Gus Johnson, Jr., recalled in the late 1970s that when he joined Eddie Vinson's band in Chicago, Dinah had been singing with the band but that Vinson had had to replace her because she was pregnant. She did, however, do a great deal of recording. During 1947, she recorded twenty-eight sides for Mercury, about half of them in Chicago with Rudy Martin's Trio, with whom she traveled often, and about half in New York with various accompanists, including Cootie Williams' Orchestra. Her pregnancy and her postdelivery layoff were not the only reason why she got to record so much that year. Maurice Petrillo, powerful head of the American Federation of Musicians, was involved in a bitter contract dispute with the major record companies and had called a strike for January 1, 1948. Six years earlier, a strike by the union in 1942–43 had paralyzed the record industry, and all the record companies were rushing to get as much material recorded as possible, for they faced an indeterminate period when they would not be able to record any music backed by live musicians, unless they went to Europe or employed instruments, such as the mouth organ, that were not on Petrillo's list of banned instruments. Their only other alternative was to ask their singers to record a cappella, and most were not willing to do so. Among the sides Dinah recorded in New York on September 20 was "Record Ban Blues."

The Petrillo ban had a strong effect on the record industry, depriving the companies, major and minor, of the opportunity to record "covers" of the songs that were hits after the ban took effect. Among their greatest tragedies was not being able to issue competitive "covers" of Nat King Cole's "Nature Boy," which was the biggest song in the country by the time of its formal release at the end of March 1948. Not that the record companies failed to try— Frank Sinatra recorded it with a vocal choir background, Sarah Vaughan and Dick Haymes sang it a cappella, the Harmonicats provided their own vocal instrumentation, and Archdale J. Jones recorded the song accompanied by a harmonica. But Perry Como refused to record the song singing a cappella, and by the time the record ban was over, many others in the recording industry had begun to share his feeling that just because a song was a hit, every singer around did not have to record it. Then, too, as a result of its long strike the musicians' union had won pay increases, and in the interest of the bottom line the record companies could no longer afford to record as many songs.

Accordingly, by the time the record ban ended, the executives of Mercury's "colored department" had realized that Dinah's talents were best utilized on blues songs to be aimed at the Negro market. She had a growing following in that market, which helped Ben Bart book her in black clubs in the major cities, though the majority of these clubs did not pay much. They were small, the heels of their clientele well worn down, and the salary for a week was often not more than enough to keep Dinah's sidemen in tow for another week. But Dinah needed the work, and the money. With the arrival of little George Jenkins, Jr., she had a son to support, not to mention a mother and two young half sisters, assorted other relatives, and a husband. "As fast as I made money, it would be gone," she later said of George Jenkins, Sr. "We just couldn't get anywhere together." Says Gordon Austin, "She found out that George was a very weak person, couldn't stand but so much. He got involved in drugs. At that time, there weren't too many musicians using drugs. They drank, but as far as pot and all, they weren't doing it. Some of them with a lot of money would fool around with cocaine, but out of fifty musicians, maybe five were doing drugs, and the rest would look down on them.'' Dinah was militantly against drugs and always let her musicians know that she would not tolerate drug use. When she found that her own husband was on drugs, she could not take it. She did not need a weak man. ''She was like a little child out there with all those wolves nipping at her heels,'' says Gordon Austin, who had lost touch with Dinah by that time, for she was based in Chicago and he was still traveling constantly. She needed someone who would help her fight them off, and George Jenkins was not that kind of man. They were divorced in July 1947.

''Then I figured I should get away from men in show business and try my childhood sweetheart,'' Dinah said years later. Robert Grayson was the son of the pastor of Saint Luke's Baptist Church where Dinah had played for the choir. The two had been ''very fond of each other'' as young teenagers, but their paths had diverged. Dinah had left Chicago to travel with Lionel Hampton, and Grayson had married. With the birth of her baby, Dinah had spent a lot of time in Chicago, and learning that Robert Grayson was free again, she'd married him.

After several years of singing on the chittlin' circuit, Dinah enjoyed returning to the world she had left behind, attending services at Saint Luke's Baptist Church and renewing old friendships in the gospel world. Grayson did not try to talk her into returning to gospel; he did not mind her being in show business. She felt that his not being in the business was a plus. He traveled with her, drove her car for her, did errands for her, at least at first. After a time, however, she decided that she needed someone else to help her, especially after she became pregnant again. There were many responsibilities attendant to a solo act: overseeing wardrobes and hairdressing, making sure that waiters and bellhops and cabbies were appropriately tipped, seeing that her gowns and her musicians' stagewear went to the dry cleaners, seeing that her car was serviced. It wasn't long before she realized that she needed a general factotum who could take care of all the details, because she couldn't afford a staff that numbered more than one. She found that all-purpose secretary-assistant-companion-wardrobe mistress-friend in LaRue Manns, who was looking for a job that would give her the opportunity to travel and meet interesting people.

LaRue had left college after a year and gone to Washington, D.C., to stay with a sister. She was working as a barmaid at the Harlem Club and was not at all happy when a friend named Georgia announced that she had just the job for LaRue. "I know a lady that's a singer and she needs someone to be a companion and friend and sister and helper, you know, everything wrapped up in one," was the way Georgia presented the job to LaRue. "She'll be here soon," Georgia continued, "The name is Dinah Washington." LaRue had never heard of Dinah Washington, but she agreed to accompany Georgia to meet Dinah when she came to town.

"She was appearing at the Club Cavern [according to Redd Foxx, the name of the club was the Crystal Cavern]," Manns recalls. "It was a beautiful club, and she was just beginning to go out on her own. We walked into the club, and she had a table prepared for us. She was up there, singing, and she just said, 'Georgia, you made it and you brought the girl along,' and kept right on singing. I learned later that she did that all the time—she could be singing and work the words that she wanted to say to people into her song and never lose a beat. That was one of the fascinating things about her talent, how she could interweave it all together. Between sets she told me that she was staying at the Dunbar Hotel and asked if I could stop by the next morning at eleven o'clock. 'I'd like to chat with you,' she said.

"So the next morning I went to her room, and when she came to the door, she said, 'One thing I like about you—you're on time.' She asked me to do a few things for her, and I said I'd be glad to before I went to work. She said, 'Well, I like you already. How would you like to go out for a two-week trial?' I said I'd talk it over with my sister and with my boss, and she said she'd talk to my boss herself if I couldn't convince him. However, this is what happened: I went to New York with her. It was a month later when I realized that I was only supposed to stay two weeks. We hit it off. We got along. I knew what I had to do for her. She hadn't gotten hip to fashions and dressing to any extent, though she knew enough to get on stage. We went shopping together. We went to the movies, everything. She was pregnant at the time, and I knew how to deal with pregnant people because I had several sisters who'd had babies."

LaRue traveled with Dinah for several months, doing mostly one-nighters, driving from place to place. "She was taking engagements for like two hundred and fifty dollars a night, or five hundred dollars for two nights, and she'd get it in one lump sum," says Manns. She spent it as fast as it came in, often on "hot" clothes that she had specially ordered from female boosters. She had boosters in just about every town where she performed, and what she bought that she could not use herself she would sell to other female performers in the next town. All this was a new experience to LaRue, as was the traveling, but Dinah was accustomed to it. "She'd been over those same roads before, with the big band," says Manns. Thus, Dinah knew pretty well where she could and could not stay, or eat. They usually stayed in boardinghouses or private homes. "The office would say we could stay at this place or that place," says Manns. She remembers one occasion, however, when they were traveling in the South, when they slept in the car. "It was from about four o'clock until daylight. We were tired

and we were running low on gas, and we didn't know where
we were going. We didn't want to run into any problems
or get shot at. So we slept in the car until it was light enough
to find a phone. And when it got to be daylight, we realized
we were sitting right in front of the house where we were
supposed to be staying." LaRue grew accustomed to being
directed to southern outhouses because public restrooms
were off-limits. She knew better than to go into most restaurants, though she recalls a time when she went into a
drugstore for ice cream and was served in inimitable red-
neck style.

"They had an ice-cream soda fountain. Dinah had said,
'You may have a problem in there. But if they say anything,
just pay for the ice cream and come out.' I went in through
the main door. The people didn't wait on me. I said, 'I'd
like to have two vanilla ice creams.' Finally, one said something to the other, and he came over to me and said, 'Ah,
you're not supposed to come through that door.' I said,
'Well, I'm not from here. I didn't know.' He said, 'You
must be from up North.' Then they look out the window
and they see this car sitting out there, you know, with New
York license plates. They gave me two scoops of chocolate.
I said, 'No, I asked for vanilla.' They said, 'We're all out
of vanilla. Take this or nothing at all.' I started out the same
way I'd come in, but they stopped me: 'No, you have to
go out the back door.' I went out the back and came around
front and got into the car. Dinah said, 'What did they give
you?' I said, 'Chocolate.' So we took that chocolate ice
cream and threw it down on the street and drove away.

"Those were the days when in the South and Midwest
there would be a rope drawn through the club to separate
the blacks and the whites; you couldn't dance together.
Nobody could cross that rope. And that was really something
to me, because I was still young and didn't know about all
that."

Dinah knew about it and took it, because the majority

of her fans were in the South. They were the ones who screamed when she sang, who greeted her with a fervor akin to worship, who threw dollar bills at her feet and pressed coins into her hands and whispered "God bless you, Sister!" Ben Bart had every intention of continuing to exploit Dinah's popularity in the South, and Dinah's own soul needed the nourishment that southern audiences seemed to be able to give her best.

In July 1948, about a month before Dinah was due to give birth to her second child, she returned to Chicago. By this time she had bought a two-family house for her mother and her two half sisters, Clarissa and Estrellita. LaRue accompanied her, and after the birth of Robert Grayson, Jr., in August, remained in Chicago with Dinah's mother, helping to care for the two boys. "Clarissa and Estrellita were very young," says Manns. "Bobby was born in the house that she had bought for her mother. We stayed there, and when she was able to go back on the road, I stayed there to help her mother with Bobby, the baby, and George, who was still a baby almost. He wasn't talking yet; in fact, I started him to putting words together and talking and also getting used to taking a bath, because he hated water and would fight every time. But I got so I would play with him and he would finally come on. I stayed there about six months, then I told her, 'Dinah, it's time for me to move on now [leave Chicago and her duties as nursemaid], cause I'm real tired.' There was a lot of pressure on me. The mother didn't want any outside help to come in, figured that Dinah's paying me, I'm supposed to do it all.''

By the time LaRue rejoined Dinah, she could see that there was a difference in Dinah's career. Because of her recording successes, Dinah was now a star, at least in the race market. Any crossover into the white market was not possible for her, given the type of material she sang. Billy Eckstine had managed that crossover. So had Nat King Cole, especially with "Nature Boy," which was number one on

the pop charts in 1948. But blues recordings were still identified as ''race'' music.

Dinah took her earnings and put a downpayment on an
apartment building at 1518 South Trumbull Avenue in Chicago. ''She gave her father and his then wife a free apartment to take care of the house,'' says Manns. ''He kept the
place there, they lived there, and whenever we went to
Chicago for a holiday or an engagement, we had somewhere
to stay and didn't have to stay in a hotel. We just moved
into the apartment building.'' Dinah did not get along well
enough with her mother to stay in her mother's house. By
the same token, she didn't get along very well with her
father, either. ''They were too much alike,'' says Manns.
''They didn't agree on anything. With her making the money,
she felt that she should have the say-so all the time. Then
the father would say, 'Well, I'm your father, and I should
do this.' She'd say, 'You ain't working.' They'd have terrible fights, and she'd call the police in a minute. It was
well known in Chicago. They'd say, 'Dinah coming? She
and her father? I guess all the police force will be out there.'
You know, same old stuff.''

Despite her problems with her family, Dinah took care
of them. She didn't just give them transient things, she gave
them roofs over their heads. At the same time, she was
building equity and tax deductions. Dinah had a fairly good
head for business when she wanted to, and she had a feeling
that the best place for profits was in real estate. Perhaps
Mahalia Jackson advised her, for Mahalia was putting her
own profits into real estate and businesses.

The record ban had been lifted in 1948 and Dinah had
recorded several sides in New York at the Royal Roost with
the Count Basie Orchestra and the Dizzy Gillespie Orchestra. She returned to New York in early 1949 to record two
sides with Mitch Miller's Orchestra—''Am I Really Sorry''
and ''I Challenge Your Kiss.'' Also in New York, in March

and May, she recorded a number of sides with Teddy Stewart's Orchestra. Stewart, who had been Gillespie's drummer, was her latest flame, and she had elevated him to orchestra leader for the session. She was separated from Robert Grayson by that time, for she had learned that he was seeing another woman. "One day an old lady who told fortunes called me in to read my fortune," Dinah recalled later. "Among other things, she told me my husband had a girlfriend, and that when I found out where she lived, I'd crack my sides laughing. From a phone number which my husband left on a table I tracked down this girlfriend, using an old trick on the telephone, and discovered she lived in front of my mother-in-law's house. The fortune-teller wasn't wrong."

The variety of songs Dinah sang in the recording sessions of early 1949 is illustrative of her versatility. "How Deep Is the Ocean," "New York, Chicago, and Los Angeles," and "Harbor Lights" were pop songs and covers of hits by white singers. "Good Daddy Blues," "Baby Get Lost," "Fast Movin' Mama," "Juice Head Man of Mine," and "Shuckin' and Jivin'" were blues songs. Still, there was little chance that they would be heard by white listeners. By the middle of 1949, however, the music industry began to pay lip service to the postwar movement against the blatant segregation that labeled records by blacks "race records." In its June 25, 1949, issue *Billboard* officially put that term to rest, retitling its "Top 15 Best-Selling Race Records" chart "Rhythm and Blues." The new term had been used informally for some time, and while it can be said that the change in terminology was simply a matter of substituting a more acceptable euphemism for the word *black,* it also described a particular form of urban black music. Dinah had the distinction of being among the first artists on that new chart, along with Roy Brown, T-Bone Walker, Bull Moose Jackson, and Winonie Harris.

On July 22, 1949, "Baby Get Lost," which she had
recorded the previous March, entered the Rhythm and Blues
charts; eventually it reached number one. Less than a month
later, "Long John Blues," which was on the flip side of
"Baby Get Lost," entered the Rhythm and Blues charts
and would climb to number twelve. That song had actually
been recorded back in September 1947, and a reason often
given for its tardy release was the 1948 record ban. But
Leonard Feather, who originally self-published "Baby Get
Lost" under a pseudonym, reasons that "Long John Blues"
might have been considered too suggestive. "It's about a
visit to the dentist—you know, 'He told me not to worry,
that my cavity just needed filling'—and I think that's what
people were really buying but maybe were ashamed to ask
for it, so they asked for 'Baby Get Lost,' which was on the
other side. But whatever the reason, 'Baby Get Lost' was
a phenomenal hit for me. It actually got up to number one,
and I didn't even have a publisher. I just published it myself;
I had no organization. And this happened while I was in
the hospital after being knocked down by a car. I was told
at that time that Dinah Washington paid my hospital expenses, and she really did, because during the time I was
in the hospital, I got a big royalty check." By the fall of
1949, Dinah Washington was a certified star and earning
top billing at the Apollo in her own right.

She treated her audiences to a varied program. Wrote
the reviewer for *Variety:* "Uninhibited as a rule, the buxom
Miss Washington is considerably toned down in chirping
the sedate 'Without a Song' and shows restraint on several
others. However, she doesn't disappoint her followers and
whams across with a suggestive tune, 'The Dentist's Song'
('You Thrill Me When You Drill Me'), for a rousing finale." Dinah appeared during that engagement with the
Ravens, a black singing quartet that recorded for National
and had a respectable string of not-quite-black versions of

standard songs like "Wagon Wheels" and "Deep Purple" and "September Song" and cover records of current pop hits like "Someday (I'll Want You to Want Me)." Later, she appeared with them at the Strand in New York and went on tour with them. They were also managed by Ben Bart, who had recorded them on his Hub label without success back in the mid-forties, and while they were successful in their own right, that was not always the case with the acts Bart booked behind Dinah. "Ben Bart used to carry everybody he had in his office off of Dinah," says Jimmy Cobb, who joined her in 1950. "Someone would call up and ask for Dinah, and we wouldn't be working. But he'd say, 'Well, Dinah won't be free until two to three months from now, but if you get her, you have to give me so-and-so under the table.' " By most accounts, Dinah did not mind appearing with Bart's less successful acts. Later on, she became well known for giving other performers a break. But in the early years she was not always as charitable to other performers as her later legend would have it. Vocalist Jimmy Witherspoon told Stanley Dance, author of *The World of Count Basie*, that Dinah had not been at all generous to him when he got his first chance to play the Regal Theater in Chicago around that time. "I never forget the first theater date I played. I had been looking forward to it for a year and a half. It was at the Regal Theater in Chicago, and Dinah Washington and the Ravens were also on the bill. They went to the manager and said there was too much singing, so they cut me off the show. It was the biggest disappointment, and Jay [McShann, the bandleader with whom Witherspoon was often appearing at this time] couldn't do anything about it. All I'd been doing was opening the show; Dinah was the star. Years later, when I'd gone out on my own, I had the pleasure of working on the same bill with her in Chicago. I called Jay McShann in Kansas City and said, 'Jay, this is the first time I ever had any vindictive thoughts about an entertainer, and I'm going to stop this show if I have to crawl on my knees!' 'Who is the entertainer?' he asked. 'Dinah, and I'm opening up in front of her.' 'Good.' he said. 'Go ahead.' She was a great talent, and I never did mention that she'd been responsible for one of the biggest hurts I ever had; but I think she sensed how I felt. She introduced me in the second show by saying, 'Ladies and gentlemen, now the male star of our show . . . !' ''

At least Ben Bart was getting her more gigs in New York, and for more money, and Dinah felt she could take a permanent suite in the Teresa Hotel, the best hotel in Harlem at the time. It wasn't big enough for the boys, who were still with Dinah's mother in Chicago, but it was a nice, spacious suite, and there was room for LaRue. Still, it was not big enough to accommodate the Amana freezer she was given on the *Tennessee Ernie Ford Show* one time. "You know how they used to give you things on those programs," says Slappy White. "She didn't have room for it, but there it sat in the apartment." During a layover in New York, White volunteered to repaint her suite at the Teresa. He knew he wasn't going to get paid for the work, since "Dinah had no money, just that Amana freezer." In between stints at the brush, White visited a new bar and restaurant that heavyweight boxer Sugar Ray Robinson had opened. Robinson did not have a proper freezer, in White's opinion, so he suggested that Dinah sell Robinson her Amana. "So, he made a deal with Dinah to buy this Amana freezer. So I go get Sandman Sims, who used to do the sand dance, and we push the freezer out of Dinah's suite, down the hall, onto the elevator, through the lobby, out to the street, down Seventh Avenue right down to Ray Robinson's restaurant. That was the type of woman she was, she didn't care. It didn't faze her that two guys were moving her freezer down to Seventh Avenue. Ray paid her for the freezer. I don't think anybody in Harlem had a big Amana freezer in their restaurant, and that was a big break for Ray Robinson.''

That fall, Dinah's recording of "Good Daddy Blues" entered the R&B charts (and would reach number nine). She was getting more booking offers and relied greatly on LaRue for help in handling her increasingly complex affairs. "She always had an agent, but I interceded as far as the contracts went. I made sure the contracts were right,'' says Manns. "I worked in the capacity of a business manager.''

LaRue also continued to advise Dinah on her clothes and stage appearance. "She had many, many wigs,'' says Manns. "She started that fad for wigs in Harlem, because you never saw them until after she made the rounds of the Harlem bars and club spots. And then I suggested that she get her hair cut short, and she started that fashion, too. I would say that she was the first star in Harlem to start having her hair straightened, or processed. Wearing her hair short, straight and short—she liked that.

"In wardrobe, she always wanted to outdo everyone else. She'd buy new pieces and put attachments on them when she went onstage. In the streets, we could look bummish if we wanted to, but she always got the preseason clothes so she would be ahead of everyone else. She would try to get sample pieces if she could, and she would always get me a few outfits along with hers. She would always say that I was so good to her and helped her out in so many ways that money didn't reward me. She could never pay me the kind of money she wanted to, so she made it up with gifts and things.

"I would say that from the beginning, even though the salary was small, I was paid well. At that time, I could do as much with that small salary as I could with a big salary now, because the money she paid me was my money. I lived with her, I had no food expenses. Clothes to be cleaned went to the cleaners with hers; of course, I did all the handwashing, hers and mine together. If I had to go home to visit the family, or if there was sickness or death in my family, she paid the way. She was generous. She had a heart as big as a whole building.''

Dinah also had an overdeveloped sense of being used, and sometimes this would sour her generosity. LaRue believes that Dinah, who throughout her life and career was privately generous to a fault, sometimes wanted the rest of the world to know the extent of her generosity. "Say, for instance, you were going someplace with her. She'd invite you to stop by her place. You'd stop by and she'd look at you and say, 'Hey, I think I've got something that would look nice on you.' You might have on a gorgeous outfit, but you would put on something she offered because she offered it. She was the authority on clothes—right?—and she was going to 'let' you wear it. She'd put a mink stole on you, or maybe some jewelry. Then you would all go out and have dinner, maybe take in a show. Afterward, after she'd had a couple of drinks, she'd sit there and look around and say, 'Hey, don't nobody burn that mink, 'cause it's mine.' Or, 'Don't lose those earrings if you feel yourself getting high.' And she's already high. That would cut right through you. She'd do this kind of thing. She'd want everybody to know. Yet, on another level, she didn't want you to let people know how generous she was.''

Dinah gave, in order to possess. The slightest threat to her possessiveness effectively neutralized her generosity.

Dinah also had a temper as short as one of the hairs on her fashionably close-cropped head. "She fired LaRue about every twenty minutes,'' says Slappy White. She also fired assorted hairdressers, musicians, and aides-de-camp with regularity; but if you knew Dinah, you didn't pay any attention. Says Slappy White, "Five minutes later, she'd look around and say, 'Where's LaRue?' '' Says LaRue, and everyone else who knew her, "She had a temper; she got mad a lot.''

But LaRue also realized that Dinah had a lot to be mad

about, and a lot of pressures on her. Despite her steadily increasing income—$15,000 in 1946, $45,000 in 1947, $75,000 in 1948, and $100,000 in 1949—she had equally increasing responsibilities. "She had the car payments to pay, and she sent money home to her mother. She was always sending money home to her family. She used to say to me, 'You know, I feel closer to you than I do to my own sisters. They never pick up the phone and say, "Hi, Ruth, how're you feeling?" or "I'm going to send you a present." ' She'd say, 'It isn't what they'd send, but it's the thought.' On her birthday or Christmas, if they could have sent her something, she would have felt as if they loved her. But it was always, 'What are you sending me for Christmas? I need money for this. I need money for that.' They didn't care how she felt."

Dinah also had to contend with the pressures of stardom and with the inevitable comparisons with Bessie Smith, whom Dinah resembled somewhat in appearance, as well as in style. Old-timers who were nostalgic for Bessie kept looking for a new Bessie in Dinah. And none other than John Hammond, record producer and star-finder, said, "Dinah's stage behavior is very similar to Bessie's. I am struck by it each time I hear her sing. [But] she's no Bessie, not yet." Dinah knew that there were other, private comparisons between her and Bessie—that they were both unattractive, rough-hewn, and moody—and she disliked the comparisons, good and bad. Still, there were bases for them.

Dinah had a volatile personality. She was rarely calm, and lived her life on the edge of one extreme emotion or another. She was deeply generous, deeply loving, capable of the greatest feelings of inferiority and of the greatest exhibitions of unfairness. Anyone who remained with her found it best not to try to figure her out, simply to learn to recognize the danger signs.

On the Road

ERNESTINE McClendon, longtime entertainment industry agent and performer, remembers meeting Dinah backstage at the Apollo in the early 1950s, through her husband who was "a straight man to all the big comics like Pigmeat Markham and the emcee at all the amateur shows at the Apollo. He worked with her, he was on shows with her, and emceed shows that she was on and he wasn't. She was just like the songs she used to sing—'I'm mean and evil, even rain don't fall on me.' If she didn't like you, she would cuss you out in a minute. That's the reason she and my husband got along so, they were alike in many ways. Very straightforward. You wouldn't want to tell a lie to her because she could see right through you. She'd just look at you, you know. Sometimes she wouldn't have to say a word, just look. With Dinah, you could tell if she didn't like you, she just wouldn't bother with you, wouldn't have nothing to do with you. That's the way Dinah was. And she would be straightforward and tell you what she felt whether you liked it or not, but she didn't hold anything against you. If you held it, that was your problem, you know? My husband liked Billie Holiday, too. He'd say about Dinah and Billie, 'They're not phony. They will give you the shirt off their backs if they like you and you need it.'

"But they wouldn't take anything off anybody. Dinah used to really be able to control those Apollo audiences. If they were making too much noise, she'd stop dead and say, 'Well, when you stop, I'll start.' And she'd just stand there and wait until the place got silent. Just recently I was doing a show at Marla's [in Los Angeles], and there were these people over at the bar, talking, and I said, 'Quiet!' But Dinah didn't holler like that. She was just as calm, didn't get angry, or at least she didn't show it. And they would quiet down, even Apollo audiences would quiet down for Dinah.

"We used to give big New Year's Eve parties, for a mixed crowd. They'd last for two days, and my husband would do all the cooking. One time there was a girl eating up all of the chicken. Dinah was in the kitchen with her and George, and this girl asks George, 'Ummm, how did you make this chicken so good?' And Dinah says, 'George takes Ernestine's G-strap and he stews it up with onions and peppers and salt and then he seasons the chicken with it.' And the girl says, 'Well, I don't give a damn. It sure is good.' "

McClendon recalls several instances of Dinah making sharp remarks to people who were overindulging in George McClendon's cooking. Perhaps that was because Dinah herself enjoyed George's cooking and couldn't have as much of it as she wanted. "She was always dieting. She'd say, 'Oh, God, I can just smell food and get fat.' "

At the time, Dinah's weight was really bothering her. LaRue Manns recalls, "After she had her last baby, she gained an awful lot of weight, and she didn't like that. She always said she had no shape. She knew she had pretty hands and pretty feet, and she could make her face look pretty. She always dreamed of being a glamour girl, and when she got into the money, she would buy very expensive clothes and waist cinchers to give her the shape that she wanted to have. And I always told her how gorgeous she was and how good she looked. But she didn't like her body. She would look at me sometimes and say, 'If I had your body and my voice, I'd be a bitch, wouldn't I?' "

She tried to downplay her girth by wearing severely tailored suits (she had twenty of them in her wardrobe at this time), simple gowns (thirty of them), and a short, simple hairstyle. But *Ebony,* which ran its first major article on Dinah in June 1950, still referred to her as "plump, good-natured Dinah" in its text and captioned one, ant's-eye view of her, "Sweater girl is role Dinah fills amply in playful mood." Still, to be featured in *Ebony* meant that Dinah had arrived, and the almost unrelievedly laudatory article no doubt pleased her.

Nineteen fifty was a watershed year for Dinah. She had four more records on the R&B charts: "I Only Know," "It Isn't Fair," and "I Wanna Be Loved," all reached number five, and in late September "I'll Never Be Free" reached number three. According to *Ebony,* her records had sold well over 2 million copies, and "Am I Asking Too Much" was close to the million mark in sales, though most discographies list the song, recorded in New York on October 16, 1948, with the Dizzy Gillespie Orchestra as unissued. Interestingly, in an August 1951 article, *Ebony* states that Dinah's song "Tell Me Why," listed in discographies as having been recorded in late 1951 or 1952, was a hit. *Ebony* kept track of the Sepia Song Hit Parade, where "Time Out for Tears," recorded in New York in 1950, held sway for thirty-two weeks. She was Mercury's best-selling artist in the Negro market, and not just on ghetto jukeboxes but in middle-class black homes, as Ernestine McClendon and Dick "Night Train" Lane will attest. Says McClendon, "Nobody could top her. Little Esther [Phillips] was the closest thing to her, and Nancy Wilson tries, but nobody can really reach out and get what she had, not her style. Her enunciation was so clear. My husband used to say, 'You listen at her, her and Ella [Fitzgerald]. You can. It's not mumble jumble, you can hear every word they say.' And then her whole interpretation—nobody else could give you the same feeling. Lady Day had her way of singing, a way of making you feel certain things, but Dinah was the queen of them all. Sometimes I get home upset and I just put on her records.''

Dick Lane, former football star and Dinah's last husband, first came to know Dinah through her records and through his wife's obsession with them. ''My first wife was an alcoholic, but I didn't know it. I married her out of the army—she was a WAC [Lane served in the army for three years and was discharged in 1952, the same year he joined the Los Angeles Rams football team]. I would come home and she would be there with all the lights out in the house, and I wouldn't even think she was home. But I could hear Dinah, real low, just barely. I would turn on the lights and say, 'Geraldine, what is it? Why are you in here with the lights out, listening to Dinah and crying?' And she'd say, 'Oh, baby, this gal just sings right to you.' I'd say, 'Girl, if you don't fix me some dinner . . .' I didn't realize how many hundreds of thousands of other people were sitting behind closed doors, with whatever their problems were, with Dinah, how she could take a song and sing it to all those people and really make them feel that they shouldn't be lonely because they had her. I didn't realize that until I got involved with her. Then other people told me that. They'd say, 'Whenever I feel like my luck is going bad, I go over there and turn Dinah on. My luck change.' ''

Mercury may not have known about the Ernestines and the Geraldines, but the company knew about the sales of Dinah's records, and when her contract came up for renewal, they offered her a contract with a comparatively big advance and presented her with a white mink as an added incentive to sign with the company for another three years. ''In those days, twenty thousand dollars was a lot of money,'' says Slappy White. ''But Dinah deserved it. She was Queen of the Jukeboxes. Every month, it was Dinah and Louis Jordan on the jukeboxes. So, when she got this big record contract, she decided to go on a tour, and she took me on, me and Redd Foxx.''

By that time, Slappy White and Redd Foxx had teamed up as Foxx and White. They often appeared on the same bill with Dinah, and sometimes she took one or the other with her for a gig. Some people recall that the two comedians alternated quite regularly in Dinah's entourage, but Slappy White was far more likely to appear with her than Foxx because Foxx's material tended to the blue.

''She didn't want Redd Foxx at first because Redd was telling dirty jokes at that particular time, and she didn't want that,'' says White. ''I told her I'd write the act out, and I did, and when she was satisfied that it was a clean act, she took us on tour with her.'' They played one-nighters here and there until they reached St. Louis, where after an engagement at the Riviera Club, Dinah went off to play some one-nighters on her own. She did not have the influence to demand that clubs pay her comedians, and there were many clubs and dance halls that could afford only Dinah and a couple of musicians.

While her new record contract hardly made Dinah wealthy, she had enough money to attract Walter Buchanan, a bass player from Pittsburgh. By this time Teddy Stewart was out of the picture, and as was her habit, Dinah installed her new husband as her bandleader. In February 1951 she recorded in New York with ''Walter Buchanan's Orchestra,'' adding his name to the studio orchestra and insisting that he receive top billing. That recording session may have been the only time Walter Buchanan ever headed a recording orchestra.

Wynton Kelly may have been with Dinah by that time.

Although his name does not appear on lists of her recordings until June 1951, William "Keter" Betts, who met Dinah "very early in '51," says that Kelly was with her then. Born in Jamaica and reared in Brooklyn, Kelly was a pianistic genius, though he never did learn to read music. He'd started working professionally at age twelve, and according to another Brooklyn pianist, Randy Weston, he was "already a fantastic pianist at the age of fifteen" and a veteran of all kinds of bar bands. He was only eighteen or nineteen when he joined Dinah. He was also epileptic, but according to Keter Betts, that didn't make much difference to anyone. "He had medicine. And he generally had someone traveling with him, and if [a seizure] ever came about, Dinah or someone knew what to do with the spoon. I don't remember him ever having a seizure on stage." Kelly was with Dinah off and on for five or six impassioned years, for theirs was a volatile relationship. Jimmy Cobb, who with Betts joined Dinah in late 1951, describes it as "a love-hate relationship."

"I don't know what they would do to tick each other off, but he was always leaving and coming back. There was a little guy who used to come to the Apollo Theater, a jeweler [LaRue Manns says his name was George Ungar]. You could give him an order to have some jewelry made, and one time she had a set of gold piano cufflinks made for Wynton, and she had something that looked like a gold record made for me. But between the time she ordered them and the time they were ready, she fell out with Wynton. So she had the man put my initials on them instead of Wynton's and gave them to me. She said, 'I'm not gonna give that blankety-blank nothing.' So I got two sets of cufflinks. I have them to this day. They're probably too heavy to wear. The cufflinks that were supposed to be his look like a grand piano, and the top opens up, so he missed a good little trinket.''

Cobb, a native of Washington, D.C., had first gone on the road with Earl Bostic's Band, thanks to the influence of his friend, Keter Betts, a bass player out of Port Washington, New York, who was with Bostic at the time. "I left Washington and met up with Earl at 125th Street and Saint Nicholas Avenue [in Harlem]," says Cobb, "and then we went and did a gig, I don't remember where. And in that first year, I remember we went back and forth to California, in a car, three times, cross-country doing jobs." Cobb was making twenty dollars a night and was paid in one-dollar bills, but it wasn't the money that mattered so much as the thrill of traveling with a band and meeting up on the road with most of the best black musicians in the country. It was a time when there were fifteen to twenty big bands, each of them with a roster of at least fifteen musicians—Lucky Millinder's, Duke Ellington's, Lionel Hampton's, Jimmy Lunceford's, Budd Johnson's, Erskine Hawkins's, Fats Wallers's, Louis Armstrong's, Luis Russell's, Earl Bostic's, and many more. Small wonder that Dinah Washington learned how to pick and choose her recording musicians. It was during his first year with Earl Bostic's band, around 1950–51, that Cobb met Dinah, who was about five years older than he. "She was a companion attraction somewhere on one of those one-nighters we were doing. It was someplace in the South, I think, or whatever route was happening at the time for those kinds of bands. It could have been on the way to Pittsburgh or Ohio or anyplace. She was traveling with just a piano player, Wynton Kelly, and our rhythm section had to play with her. So the bass player, Keter, and the drummer, me, made a trio behind her."

According to Keter Betts, the place where they first met was Wildwood, New Jersey. "She was traveling with just a piano player, Wynton, and played with the various bands out of the office—we were working out of Ben Bart's office then. We hit it off real good, and one thing led to another and we became friends. Then, later on, the Bostic band was in Wildwood for the whole summer. She came down there and spent a month, brought her sons."

After that, says Cobb, "We were all on tour together for about three or four months, and I don't know, it just evolved into a relationship. So, we used to travel in different cars and after we got together, I started to travel with her. One night I almost missed a job because of some blockade on the highway. I got there late, and Earl Bostic was upset. It got kinda weird, me traveling with her and playing with his band, so Keter and I left the band and started traveling with Dinah as part of her trio."

During that tour, Dinah split with Walter Buchanan. "I was there when they broke up," says Keter Betts. "It's a long story." But it was a very short marriage, a mere few months. "In no time at all I realized the marriage was doomed," Dinah told Dave Hepburn for the article, "Me and My Six Husbands." "I considered it a joke when he told me one day he wanted a new car and he was going down to pick one out. But I was laughing through my teeth. 'While you're there,' I said, 'get one for me too.' Of course we got no car. As Fate would have it, I called him at his father's one night, and after our conversation he hung up the telephone. I was about to hang up my phone when, by the sound coming through, I realized his phone was off the hook. There was a loud laugh, and I heard someone say, 'You better stay with this woman and get all the money you can.' That was enough for me. Bursting with anger I . . . told him I wanted a divorce. He had the gall to sue me for alimony, but when I told the story to the judge, he dismissed the case."

Dinah turned her attentions to her young trio. Says Betts, "When I went with Bostic, I was the youngest guy in the band—I was going on twenty-one, but I was twenty. Then, a few years later, I went with Dinah and I'm the oldest guy in the band and I'm just twenty-three. So I got pushed into adulthood quick. I was the oldest guy—Wynton was nineteen.

"From the time I went with Dinah, she put me in charge of the two cars. I would make sure that they got grease jobs, oil changes, and all that periodically. And I was driving one and I kept one all the time. She was buying two new cars every year because we were putting on over one hundred thousand miles. Chryslers were my preference, but she liked them, too. We had a Cadillac limo once, we had DeSoto station wagons; when I went with her, she had a Buick and something else. But it turned out that Chryslers were better, more durable cars, especially at that time. I would map out the route of where we were going, and by the time I was with her a year or two, I didn't even have to look at the map, I knew this country straight, what route to take and everything. But I would map out the route for whoever was driving the other car in case we got lost."

Cobb remembers, "There was a car in front, and then a station wagon with a U-haul behind. I think at one point we had two station wagons that were crammed full of everything—all the household stuff we needed, the instruments, her wardrobe, she had a suitcase with three hundred pairs of shoes in it. The station wagon was usually a Chrysler—those were the ones she liked. I think I learned to drive out there on the road—everybody had to help out with the driving because we usually had to drive a long, long way. In the South, there were a lot of places you couldn't stop, they had White Only signs everywhere, and it was really segregated to the hilt. We stayed in a lot of private homes, in hotels where we could, but most of the time we just tried to get in and get out and go on to the next town that might have a decent motel or something. In the South, we'd play small theaters where they usually showed movies, black places."

Although it is difficult to understand, from the perspective of the 1980s, how black musicians could undergo such humiliation and still function, it was not usual for blacks to protest discrimination. It was just one more indignity of the road, and when you were on the road for months at a time, you didn't distinguish between indignities. "We'd get the itinerary and look at it, and there would be ninety-nine one-niters. That's in three months," says Slappy White. "We might have three days off here, two off there, but that was all across the country."

Dinah and her entourage played the chittlin' circuit, theaters in ghettos across the country, the Howard in Washington, the Royal in Baltimore, the Earle in Philadelphia, the Apollo in New York, the Regal in Chicago, and a seemingly endless series of other theaters in the Midwest and West. "Dinah was ahead of her time," says Redd Foxx, who occasionally alternated with Slappy White as Dinah's opening act during these years. "She wouldn't sing white, and because of that, she couldn't get the big, downtown jobs. She wound up at the Club Alabam on Central Avenue in Los Angeles." Still, according to Foxx, his first big break came in 1951 when he traveled to California with Dinah for a two-week stint. During that same West Coast stint, in December 1951, Jimmy Cobb also got a break and was first elevated to the position of orchestra leader.

They were playing the Tiffany, at Eighth and Normandie in Los Angeles, and Cobb considered it a nice theater. So did *Ebony,* which mentioned that Dinah played it for the first time that year and that the "mixed audience" yelled for more. She played six shows a night, seven days a week for two weeks. Slappy White, who was on the bill as the comedian, however, regarded it as too small to be lucrative: "The joint don't sit but eighty-six people, so how much money can you make if a joint sits eighty-six people and it's the number-one joint in town?" But for Cobb, it represented a big break. "Dinah just put my name in front of

the house orchestra,'' Cobb explains. But that led to a chance
to record. In Los Angeles they recorded four sides: "Trouble
in Mind,'' "Wheel of Fortune,'' "Tell Me Why,'' and
"When the Sun Goes Down.'' Both "Wheel of Fortune''
and "Trouble in Mind'' had reached the R&B charts by the
spring, and Leonard Feather, who was now writing for
Down Beat, took the occasion to devote an article to her,
extolling her versatility as: "a gal who can sell in six figures
on 'The Wheel of Fortune' and turn around and make a
superb 'Trouble in Mind.' When they recorded her with
strings recently, one tune that Dinah chose was 'I Can't
Face the Music'—the very song with which, as an unknown
15-year-old, she began her career by winning an amateur
contest in Chicago. For little Ruthie Jones, the wheel of
fortune has come full circle.'' Feather had other, personal
reasons, to be proud of Dinah. That spring, in Chicago,
with the "Jimmy Cobb Quintet,'' she recorded his composition, "Blowtop Blues,'' again, and within a month "New
Blowtop Blues'' was number seven on the charts.

Dinah and Jimmy Cobb had a nice working relationship,
as she had with almost all musicians. There was a mutual
respect that came through in the music they made, whether
on stage or in a recording studio. Dinah was not easy to
work with. She would dress down a musician in a minute,
and she didn't care who heard it, if she thought he wasn't
playing as he should. "Dinah had perfect pitch,'' says Slappy
White. "We were at a record session one day, and Dinah
was singing, and all of a sudden she stopped. She said,
'Clark Terry, your treble is flat,' and he later admitted to
me that it was. When we were on the road, sometimes she'd
get hoarse, and when she did, she'd switch keys so fast you
had to be a very skilled piano player to keep up with her.
Wynton Kelly could do that, and he worked with her so
long he could tell when she was going to switch keys even
before she did it.''

After a time, Jimmy Cobb and Keter Betts could do the same, and perhaps the finest relationship Dinah had with a group of musicians was that which she and her young trio, Kelly, Cobb, and Betts, enjoyed. Says Betts, "As far as I'm concerned, that was the greatest thing that ever happened to me, working with her. Because I got a chance to really learn something about music. Where before then I just thought that I knew music, I mean changes and so forth, through her I got to learn to listen to the words of tunes, and all of a sudden it opened up a brand-new world. She had an eye for new talent—I think she learned that from Gladys Hampton, listening to new talent and at all times to new people. She used to take the whole trio out quite a bit. We'd go into some town and she knew of some new group or some place that had a good act, and she would take us to hear it. She would say, 'I want to take you out and show you something you haven't seen.' We'd go to Chicago, and she'd take us to the Club Delisa there, and we saw big bands and dancing girls. One night she took us to a club in New York, down in the café-society part of town, the Village, to see Mae Barnes. She'd take us out to see various unusual acts."

Dinah is credited with discovering any number of musicians, among them Paul Quinichette, a tenor saxophonist, whom she insisted back her in the recording session in Chicago in the spring of 1952 that produced "New Blowtop Blues" as well as three other sides—"Pillow Blues," "Cold, Cold Heart," and "Double Dealing Daddy." "The introduction on 'Cold, Cold Heart' was played by Paul Quinichette," says Slappy White, "and that made Paul Quinichette. She knew that he wanted to be like Lester Young, and she had an ear. If you look at Dinah's record sessions and at the type of musicians that she had, and then look at other girls' record sessions, you'll see that she had the best musicians on all her albums. She'd tell the producers who she wanted, and that's who they'd get, because they wanted her to sing, didn't they? And if she didn't have who she wanted, she wouldn't sing.''

Only in rare instances did she allow her heart to over-shadow her ear when it came to choosing sidemen and backup musicians, and Jimmy Cobb was not a musician who benefited solely from her heart. Not just her heart but her ear demanded that he be with her.

They were together for quite a while, given Dinah's track record. She later said, ''He was the sweetest, kindest and most honorable guy I had met up to then.'' When Dinah moved out of her suite at the Teresa and into an apartment at 2040 Seventh Avenue, a large apartment house between 121st and 122nd Street that was owned, according to Betts, by a Mr. Fenner and where a number of entertainers lived, Cobb moved his belongings in there, too. Theirs was a much less stormy relationship than Dinah's with Wynton Kelly, whose departure brought to an end the most long-lasting musical assemblage that Dinah had ever enjoyed.

Kelly, despite his epilepsy, went into the army in 1952. For the next two years, several piano players took his place. According to Keter Betts, a woman named Beryl Booker was the first. ''She was with us about six or seven months. She was very big in the middle forties when she was with Slam Stewart. Then we had Sleepy Anderson out of Chicago, then Junior Mance.'' Although they all missed Kelly, Dinah, Betts, and Cobb remained close, and Dinah and Cobb remained intimate. But there was little talk of marriage, which was out of character for Dinah—but given her experience with Walter Buchanan, perhaps it is understandable.

Dinah's mother remarried in 1953. Her new husband, James Kimbrough, had children of his own, creating an even larger extended family for Dinah to celebrate and worry over. ''There were ten children in the house,'' says Ferris

Kimbrough, who was sixteen when her father married Dinah's mother. "We had just moved to Chicago, and there were still two younger sisters in Mississippi, but there were five sisters and a brother in Chicago. Then there were Dinah's two kids and her two sisters and brother, so there were ten children in the house."

As Ferris Kimbrough heard it, Dinah had not been in Chicago for a long time before the Jones-Kimbrough marriage, as long as ten years. Since this was 1953 and Dinah's children were still with her mother, Ferris was misled. Dinah's mother may have bemoaned too much the frequent absences of her daughter. Dinah's mother told Dinah in no uncertain terms that she was to welcome the new members of the family. Says Ferris, "My stepmother told her on the phone, 'I've married a man, he's got five kids, and when you come home, I want you to be nice to them.' So when Dinah came home, she brought everybody presents, and the next day we went to Riverview Park. There were so many of us—the ten kids, plus her entourage of maids and hairdressers, Jimmy, other people in the band who were close to her. She cooked—she cooked forever. She had her hairdresser do all the girls' hair. She stood and watched. She was a warm, family person."

Jimmy Cobb enjoyed Dinah's family and life with Dinah. He would have liked to continue seeing a few of his other woman friends, but after he and Dinah got together, his other women friends seemed to disappear. "I used to wonder . . . I'd go into a club, and the female population wouldn't even get near me. I found out years later that that was Dinah's doing. I'd go back through a town and a girl would tell me, 'I wanted to talk to you, but Dinah told me that you were her man and to stay away.' " Dinah did not have much use for other women, unless she could control them.

Recalls Cobb, "One time in St. Louis, I don't remember

where we were playing, but after we got done, we went over to Pop Chambers's place. He was a black politician or something, had a lot of pull in town. He had a little bar, an afterhours place, and a lot of little girls that hung around. Dinah was sitting there, telling her jokes—she was used to being the center of attention. This one little girl wasn't paying her any mind, and Dinah got peeved. She threw a glass at her—I don't know if it was half-jokingly or not, but it hit a service-area railing and broke, and a piece of it flew off and hit this girl in the face. She was a nice-looking girl, and she got pissed. So she started at Dinah, but before they could get to each other, people pulled them back. I've often wondered if that girl didn't set something off in Dinah's head, maybe reminded her of all those light-skinned, pretty girls that made her feel like she wasn't pretty. That girl probably reminded her of that light-skinned singer who was in Lionel Hampton's band when Dinah joined up with Hampton.'' From that time on, at least according to Dinah's stepsister, Ferris Kimbrough, whenever Dinah had to play St. Louis, she kind of sneaked in quietly and got out fast.

Cobb felt that Dinah wanted him to confront the world the way she did. ''I don't know what she expected of me. She expected me to get into fights or something. A lot of times that didn't happen. We'd have conversations about that. I remember one time we were in Las Vegas and she lost all the money she had to pay us off with. We couldn't get a draw for her going to the crap tables. Usually she was pretty lucky—she'd go into a room with the fellows and crap with them and break them all sometimes. I remember one time over in the Dust Bowl where the brothers were trying to hustle, this little guy had a shack that was supposed to be a small casino. He lived in the shack and had his Cadillac parked outside. He had about three hundred in silver dollars on the table when Dinah came in and started shooting crap, and pretty soon she'd shot all the money off the table. She busted his little game. So, now he wants her to stay there while he goes and borrows some money, so he can get his money back, some kind of way. She's drunk, because all the time you're playing the guy's giving you liquor, and she says, 'Yeah, let him go and get some money.' She thinks she's gonna beat him out of that, too. I told her, 'No, Dinah, let's go. The man doesn't have any money—you've got everything he's got. Let's go, unless you want to give it back to him.' I'm pushing her out to the car, and she still wants to stay. Now she's gonna go into her pocketbook and draw a pistol on me. I get the pistol from her and we get into the car and go, but she still wants to stay. Got a sackful of this man's silver dollars and still wants to stay. If she had, she probably would have lost it, and then told me I should have made her leave.''

According to Cobb, she was drinking a lot at this time. "She loved cognac—Courvoisier—but it didn't affect her singing. The only thing that affected her singing was working too hard. All those one-nighters trying to make money because she was in debt. Her mother needed money, she needed to pay her musicians, and so a lot of jobs she shouldn't have taken she took because she needed the money. She couldn't afford to stop working. She had been having a little trouble with her throat. She went to a doctor and he said she'd strained her larynx or whatever, shouldn't sing for two-three weeks to give her throat a chance to heal. But being in debt like she was, she couldn't do that. After that, she never got quite what she had before, her voice wouldn't be as clear or as strong as it was before, she would crack in some places because when she was trying to do these little things to make people shout, her voice wasn't strong enough.''

Dinah wasn't happy singing in front of an audience unless she could make them shout, or cry, or display some emotion, and a sore throat wasn't going to stop her. Those little roadhouses and dance halls and tobacco barns might not have paid much, but they housed the people who made her feel at home, and she wanted to give them all she had. Recalls Slappy White, "One time we were working at Robert's Show Lounge [in Chicago], and she's got the house packed. Robert wants to try to get the house empty for the next show, and he's trying to tell Dinah to cut her act short. She says, 'Listen, Robert, let me tell you one thing.' This is from the middle of the stage. 'Ain't this house packed in here? You're worried about me cutting the show so you can get another packed house. The next house is going to be packed anyway. I don't care how long they wait out there, I'm not going to cut these people short.' She's got the people on her side now. She says, 'If you make me mad, you know I'll get sick, and tonight's Friday, and you don't want me to get sick Saturday and Sunday, do you?' She'd do things like that and she'd have her way."

Dinah acted the star to the hilt, and to the extreme discomfort of those around her. Ann Littles, called Big Ann, who acted as companion and manager when Dinah was on the road, was fired as often as LaRue had been. Keter Betts left a couple of times, but came back. Jimmy Cobb stayed because he loved Dinah, though her changeability was wearing thin for him. She was often depressed, often drank too much. Cobb remembers that there were suicide notes, though not addressed to him. "She left a couple for LaRue one time. I don't know if it was the influence of the cognac or depression or what. Maybe she thought that was the way a star was supposed to act. I used to try to figure out why she did these things. It didn't dawn on me until later. I was watching this Joan Crawford and Bette Davis movie, and it dawned on me that she'd been watching their movies all her life. You know, when you're poor, the best thing you can do to escape everything is to go to a movie. She must have figured she was going to be like Joan Crawford or

Bette Davis. She used to make up, try to look as close as she could get, like Bette Davis. Her eyelids and all that stuff. She tried to look like that, and she tried to act like that, too. That's how her love life went." Life had to be lived to the hilt; if there wasn't a scene, she wasn't living.

Dinah and Jimmy Cobb broke up in mid to late 1953. As Dinah put it in the article "Me and My Six Husbands," "He had another interest besides me, one of my closest girlfriends. As it turned out, he got closer and closer to this girl and further and further away from me. We decided to part, and I must admit I was hurt. But with Jimmy there was no bitterness. At least he had the guts to come to me and discuss things like a man." Cobb recalls, "She was messing around and not wanting me to do it. Then I ran across a girl who used to play piano with Arnett Cobb and we had a relationship, and one night she told me she was pregnant. I confessed to Dinah and blew her mind. So I had to move out. I went to the Teresa Hotel. But I stayed on with Dinah for a while. I didn't want to go back to Washington, so I stayed and worked and went through whatever it was I had to get through until I got to where I felt I needed to be." He backed her in a recording session in New York at which she sang "TV Is the Thing (This Year)," which went on to be a major R&B hit. The instrumentation included bongos, played by Candido Camero, because bongos were also the thing that year. "In between there someplace, I think she was trying to get us back together some way, or just have the pleasure of my . . . uh . . . attention anytime she felt like it, which was not about to happen."

Slappy White, who was privy to most of Dinah's relationships, believed that Dinah really cared about Jimmy Cobb. "She stayed with him about three-four years. They were compatible, but she was still Dinah Washington (the star). I think he stayed with her longer than anybody else."

"Yeah, Slappy," says Cobb. "He could talk her out of

anything. He would go to her and say, 'I think old Jimmy Cobb is messing around with somebody.' She'd say, 'Yeah? Who is it?' He'd give some name and then he'd say, 'Hey, Dinah, can you lend me fifty?' He'd get her when she was thinking of something else.''

Dinah's breakup with Jimmy Cobb did not prevent her from celebrating the marriage of another member of her beloved trio, Keter Betts. He recalls, ''When my wife and I got married, Dinah set the whole thing up for us. She took my wife down to Saks Fifth Avenue and bought the gown and this and that. Set up the thing at Adam Clayton Powell's church. Had a photographer for pictures. It was October 1953. Closing night at Birdland, she had a caterer come, bring food and everything, and gave a big party.''

In fact, Dinah enjoyed it all so much that she decided to stage another marriage of her own—and her first quasi-marriage of record. On November 19, 1953, she announced that she had married drummer Larry Wrice in Boston. On her return to New York a few days later, there was a large reception at Barney Josephson's Café Society Downtown. That the marriage never actually took place was beside the point. Dinah had a good time—and a man to take home with her to Chicago for Christmas.

Dinah always made a point of spending Christmas in Chicago so she could be with her sons. When she was at home, recalls Ferris Kimbrough, things were quieter than one would have expected. ''It was never really quiet around her, but knowing how mother was, things would quiet down to a certain extent. She was just like any other daughter, and as long as the subject of her going away from the church didn't come up, their relationship was pretty good. I remember that first Christmas, there wasn't a party or anything—Dinah knew not to have parties in her mother's house—but a lot of people came for Christmas dinner. She was working at the Regal Theater with the Cootie Williams

Band, and Eddie 'Cleanhead' Vinson and all those people came over. Slappy White was there. Mama was praying, and she said something about the Lord being there, and Slappy said out loud, 'Oh, I didn't know *He* was here,' and everybody around the table cracked up.''

Dinah's relationship with Larry Wrice was short-lived. According to Jimmy Cobb, so was Wrice's career as a drummer: ''Later on, I think he was a ski instructor in Aspen. Then there was Hal Mooney. He used to write arrangements for us. He hung out with us in Vegas and Los Angeles. He was a nice guy, wrote good arrangements.''

Trombone player Gus Chappell was another. A fellow alumnus of Wendell Philips High School, he and Dinah had seen each other off and on since he'd backed her on her first sides for Mercury back in January 1946. He had recorded with her in New York in June 1953, at which session were produced Dinah's first recordings for the new EmArcy label started at Mercury by Bobby Shad. While some people thought Chappell was a husband, Slappy White says that he was an ''acting husband.'' ''You got to be husband and wife to check into hotels, you know, and she'd say, 'This is my husband.' As far as the public was concerned, she was married. Married or not, she didn't never have nobody with no money.

''At the time her boyfriend was Gus Chappell, we went into Vegas—a club owned by Henry Slate and his brothers. We did one show, and then they came in and closed the man down because he didn't have a liquor license. They put some kind of seal on the door, and my best sport outfit is in there, but I can't break the seal. We didn't have anything to do for a few days, so we gambled. Me and Dinah went into a gambling joint over on the black side of town one night, and Dinah got to shooting dice and she was winning. I'm betting with her, and pretty soon I've got all

these silver dollars in my pocket. The guy warmed up to
Dinah, and pretty soon we're staying in his house. He's her
new boyfriend. Meanwhile, I've got all these silver dollars,
but I don't want anybody to know I've got money.

"We leave Vegas and our next job is in Los Angeles,
at the Oasis on Western Avenue. The second night we're
there, she and Gus Chappell get into an argument, and he
hits her with the trombone stand, hits her right across the
eye. It's just a man-woman argument, but he has to get out
of town. She has a black eye. I tell her, 'Dinah, look, since
you got the publicity, go get a white mink patch, put a white
mink patch over your eye. Be different.' She goes and gets
a white mink patch, but she can't go back to the Oasis.
That's two jobs in a row messed up.

"The next date we've got is in Chicago, so now we've
got to cross the desert, and it's short money. There's two
cars. I ride in her car—me and the maids. The band rides
in the station wagon with all the luggage. We get out in the
desert and two tires blow on the station wagon. Her money
is short, and she needs ninety to a hundred dollars for two
new tires. I tell her I'll handle it. I go in and pay for the
two tires, but I tell her the man's going to let me owe him
the money. I don't want her to know I got the money. We
get to Chicago, and she tells the guy to send the money to
this service station. I say, 'No, no, don't send nothing. Me
and that man are personal friends. Give me the money and
I'll send it to him.' She says she wants to send the money
to him directly. I say, 'Directly? You didn't get the tires
directly, the tires came through me.' It took me all day long
to convince her to give me the money, because it was all
paid. Why should I spend my money? I would loan the
musicians twenty dollars or something like that, but I wasn't
going to spend my money on tires.''

Money problems are what caused Dinah to leave Ben
Bart. There was "some discrepancy there," says Keter Betts.

"We were working the Apollo when Joe Glaser came to see her, and then later on some other stuff went down and so forth, and then we went with Joe. We went with Joe in '54 because that's when we started getting booked into a little better places. It might have been in late '53, because I know in '54 we went to New Orleans, and it was the first time that a black act had ever worked this particular club, Curley's Neutral Corner. And we went in there and they had two bands—a country and western band and a Dixieland band—and Dinah. What was unusual about that was that Al Hirt was in the Dixieland band—tall, skinny guy. I didn't see him again until I was in New York with Ella [Fitzgerald]. I knew who he was but I didn't remember him being in that band, and he came up to me and gave me a big bear hug and said, 'Don't you remember me? I was in the band when you played Curley's Neutral Corner.' Since then we always talk about that.''

Cobb remembers that booking also. ''Curley's Neutral Corner was owned by an eccentric rich guy named Dan Anthony. New Orleans was a segregated town then, but he hired whoever he wanted. The town detectives were in the club and after we came off the stage, they didn't even want us to stay there, but this guy made sure we had a table so we wouldn't have to go outside between sets. It doesn't sound like a big thing, but for that time it was.''

It was Joe Glaser who got Dinah and the trio their first booking in a white Las Vegas club, and this time it was a solid booking, not one that ended almost before it began.

One advantage to playing Las Vegas was that performers normally stayed there for at least a month, a welcome respite from the usual schedule of one-nighters. Dinah could have her children with her when she played Vegas. "She sit down for a month, she'd have those boys with her,'' says Slappy White. Nat King Cole and a few other black entertainers had broken the color barrier at white clubs like the El Rancho in the mid-forties, but according to LaRue Manns, Dinah was the first black woman. "She played the Sahara," says Manns. "This was the beginning of them putting black acts on the Strip. The Will Masterson Trio and Nat Cole and a few others had been there, but not many. She wasn't booked for the big room but for the lounge. And we couldn't stay in the hotel. They had a trailer parked next to the kitchen entrance. It was fully equipped—bedroom, living room, all the trimmings—but it wasn't the hotel. Dinah couldn't go through the main entrance. She had to go up a walk and go through the kitchen to get to the lounge stage. We could not go into the casino to play. I could go in with a white musician, but I couldn't go in there on my own or with a black guy. That was the way things were. We didn't resent it, exactly. But we looked at it this way: If we were good enough to work and perform for the people, why couldn't we then go into the casino, if we had the money and were dressed properly? I'll never forget—Kaye Ballard was in the big room, and she was more upset than we were. Between shows, she would come out and stay in the trailer with us. We'd eat, play cards, have cocktails, whatever. But Dinah said she would never go back to the Sahara again, not if that was how she was going to be treated."

Dinah liked to gamble, and in Las Vegas she wanted to gamble at the closest casino. But in those days blacks had to go across the tracks to a place called the Dust Bowl. "There was a place run by a Chinese guy," Jimmy Cobb remembers. "Later on, somebody had the heart to build a casino over there that stayed open twenty-four hours a day, because at that time the Strip closed at about three or four o'clock in the morning. After people got off work, they'd go over to the Dust Bowl. The owners on the Strip didn't like that. In fact, they told their employees that anybody caught gambling over there would be automatically fired. Eventually, they built a whole complex over there for the employees—a club, facilities for the workers to live in, all that."

Queen of the Blues

BY the time Dinah reached Chicago to spend Christmas with her family, no fewer than three of the songs she had recorded in Los Angeles the previous August with Hal Mooney's Orchestra hit the R&B charts, which came as no surprise to Bobby Shad, who'd overseen the session. It was one of those times when Dinah and the musicians just clicked. Junior Mance was on piano, Keter Betts on bass, Max Roach on drums, Clifford Johnson and Clark Terry on trumpet. In Shad's opinion, it was the best group of sides Dinah had ever cut. "I Don't Hurt Anymore" entered the charts on October 6. It was a perfect Dinah Washington blues song. Those who knew her say that she had the ability to invest her songs with personal emotion, and "I Don't Hurt Anymore" must have had particular meaning to her at a time when her comparatively long relationship with Jimmy Cobb had ended. "I don't hurt any more/All my teardrops are dried . . . No use to deny/I wanted to die the day you said we were through . . . I've forgotten somehow/That I cared so before/Yes, it's wonderful now/I don't hurt any more." "That was a big, big record for her," says Slappy White. "That record was for women. Every time she sang it, the women just screamed. We played a big show in Detroit one time, and it was Ella Fitzgerald, Mahalia Jackson, and Dinah Washington on the bill. They made a mistake and put Dinah before Mahalia and Ella. Dinah had 'I Don't Hurt Anymore' out, and when Dinah sang 'I Don't Hurt Anymore,' everybody in the audience just screamed. They would not let her off the stage. Now Ella and Mahalia got to follow this. I was just standing there watching and I couldn't believe it; she upset the whole auditorium. She had to go back and do 'I Don't Hurt Anymore' again. I've seen her stop many a show because, boy, when she went out there, she did it all.'' "Dream," the flip side of "I Don't Hurt Anymore," entered the charts one week later, on October 13, and by Christmas "Teach Me Tonight" had also hit the charts and would become almost as big a hit as "I Don't Hurt Anymore."

Her sons were about seven and six then. Dinah tried to compensate for her frequent absences by giving them lavish gifts. "She always wanted to give her children what she'd never had," says LaRue, "and they had everything. When they were seven, eight, nine years old they were out playing in the park in sixty-five- to seventy-five-dollar sweaters. She'd buy little cufflinks with diamonds and sapphires in them. I used to tell her, 'Honey, you're ruining the boys.' She'd say, 'Well, I want them to look like Dinah Washington's kids, not like average kids. But I want them to learn and live like average kids.' Anyway, I think it was too much too soon."

Dinah loved children. Child performers were especially dear to her. "She loved the Hines kids," says Manns, referring to Gregory and Maurine Hines, who in those days were performing with their father in an act called Hines, Hines, and Dad. Leslie Uggams told Ted Fox, author of *Showtime at the Apollo*, about performing at the Apollo Theater with Dinah. "Dinah Washington was very, very special. Dinah could cuss better than anybody I ever heard in my life, but she had a heart of gold. When it got real heavy, and she'd get to cussing, she'd say, 'Okay, Juan-ita,' which was my mother's name, 'take baby into the dressing room. I got some strong cuss words I gotta use here.' My mother would take me in and close the door, but Dinah's voice carried everywhere, it wasn't like you couldn't hear it.''

Little Esther Phillips was a star on the R&B charts by the time she was fifteen. Playing on her youth, her manager, Johnny Otis, dressed her up ''like a little southern girl,'' for which he was criticized by some. Recalls Otis, ''So after the first couple of shows at the Apollo, Dinah Washington comes backstage. She takes Esther with her, and brings her back with her hair done, high-heel shoes on, nylon stock-ings, and a form-fitting dress. She looked like she was thirty. Dinah Washington said, 'That's disgraceful, having her look like she's in the cotton fields.' ''

It was backstage at the Apollo that Dinah first met little Patti Austin, daughter of Gordon Austin. Austin and Dinah had lost touch over the previous few years. In the interim, Austin had married for a second time and had a daughter, Patti, who was then about four. They lived out on Long Island but would occasionally go into the city to see a show, and when Austin heard that Dinah was going to be at the Apollo, he took his wife and daughter to see her. After the first show, Patti remembers, they went backstage. ''I re-member her sitting at her dressing table when we walked into the dressing room, and my father introduced us—'This is my new wife, and this is my little girl.' She shook my mother's hand and gave her a little kiss on the cheek and then she came over to me and, being very facetious, leaned over to me and said, 'Hi, I'm Dinah Washington, and I'm a singer.' There were some people in the dressing room, and they all cracked up. I said, 'Well, I'm Patti Austin, and I'm a singer, too.' She just kind of looked at me, and then she started laughing.

''I had always sung. I would go to Woolworth's with

my mother, and she would leave me in the toy department and go do her shopping, and when she came back, there'd be a crowd of people standing around me, and I would be doing whatever was possible to the Muzak that was playing in the store. So when Dinah made this remark to me, it was as if she was opening the door for me to let somebody know, Yeah, I sing, too.

"So, not skipping too much of a beat, she said, 'Well, if you're a singer you're going to go out onstage and you're going to sing tonight.' That was fine with me. She had a piano player come in, and she asked me what I wanted to sing. I said, 'I'll sing "Teach Me Tonight" in B-flat,' and the piano player cracked up. We went to wherever the piano was and rehearsed the number, and Dinah went on and did her second show and introduced me, and I came out and sang 'Teach Me Tonight.' The trouble was, the piano player hadn't gotten the word to the band about what key to play it in. They had that tune. It was a big hit for her, and that's how I knew it, from hearing it at home. But they were used to playing it in a different key. The piano player had transposed it in his head, but he forgot to tell the band, so they started to play it in the written key, the eighth key, and by the time they had played the intro, I stopped the band. I said, 'You're playing in the wrong key,' and the entire audience went into hysterics. So they changed keys, and I did the number, and Dinah just kind of shook her head and laughed and hugged me and took me back into the wings and put me next to my parents. Then she went out and made some crack like 'Never follow children or animals,' and did the rest of the show.

"In the meantime, Sammy Davis, Jr., was rehearsing his show downstairs that night—there was a rehearsal hall under the stage—and when I stopped the band to tell them they were playing in the wrong key, someone ran down to get him. He was there, watching, when I did the number, and afterward he went over to my parents and asked if I could work with him the following week. My parents didn't know what to say. My mother looked at me and said, 'Well, it's not really up to us. It's about what Patti wants to do, though if I had my druthers, she wouldn't be doing any of this.' Of course, I was saying, Oh, boy, Oh, boy, Oh, boy! My whole career started that night.

"After Dinah finished her second show, she came back to the dressing room. She said, 'Well, that's it, I'm your godmother, and you're going to do my next revue at the Apollo. We're going to call it "The Queen of the Blues and the Princess." ' She hooked me up with George Sheck, who was a manager—I don't know if George managed her or if she just knew him. We went to Kriegsman, a place in the forties where everybody in show business used to have their professional pictures taken, and had pictures taken together. Then she took me to meet this young, up-and-coming arranger to have some charts written for this act we were going to do together, the arranger being Quincy Jones. She said, 'Go and sing for this man so he can get your keys and everything,' and I went and sang for him, and he said, 'That's it, I'm your godfather.' So, in the course of about a week I got all these godparents, and all I had to do was sing—it was a good deal.

"We rehearsed and we were ready to go and do the show; they were putting the letters up on the billboard at the Apollo when the Children's Aid Society came and said, 'Oh, no you don't. How old is this little whippersnapper?' I was underage at the time. That was an era when terrible things had happened to children in the industry—working eighteen hours a day and all that madness, kids on diet pills, which is speed by any other name, to keep them cute and adorable. The Children's Aid Society had really clamped down; they've eased up a lot since then. So, I did not get to do the show, and Dinah was devastated, much more than

I was. I was kind of kept away from the promotional end of it. I posed for pictures and I did little interviews, but I didn't really know what it was all about. I didn't know that my picture had been in the papers until years later. In the meantime, I'd done a couple of shows with Sammy. Maybe that's how the Children's Aid Society found out about me. I wasn't getting paid at that point, but I did do a couple of shows at the Apollo with him. He brought me out by saying he was going to introduce his next wife, and that had everybody at the edge of their seats because at that time he was marrying everybody. They were all dying to see who was going to come out, and here comes this little midget, even smaller than Sammy.

"Through George Sheck I started doing a show called *Star Time* on TV, which was a local New York show. It came on opposite *The Children's Hour*, which is what Leslie Uggams got started on. I think they were on Channel Nine, and we were on Channel Eleven at the same time Sunday mornings. Connie Francis and Bobby Darin both got their start on the show when I was on it. I did that for about two years. We rehearsed from Wednesday to Friday, or something like that, and my dad would take me into the city and I'd rehearse after school, and I'd go to school the next morning, all in accordance with the law. At that point I was lying about my age. I sort of laid low for a few months and then I came back and said, 'Well, I'm six now.' I was still four and a half—had a very quick birthday.

"Then I got a contract, also through Dinah, with RCA Records. At that point you didn't run in and cut an album, you cut four sides, and then if they sold, you would make an album. So I cut four sides, and RCA had this huge publicity campaign ready, and here they come again, that wonderful Children's Aid Society, and they blocked that, too. For some reason they didn't bother me on *Star Time*. While I was doing *Star Time*, I started doing another show called *Ray Bolger's Washington Square*. That was a national show, and I did that for about two years. It was a variety format, and I played one of the local kids on the show; there was a segment where he did a number with four or five kids every week, and I was one of those kids. So all that came about as a result of Dinah's interest in me, and she just kind of mother-henned me to death and pushed me wherever she could."

Dinah was equally interested in the young Quincy Jones, with whom she felt both a geographical and a musical kinship. Jones had been born in Chicago, though his family had moved to the Seattle area when he was ten. He had also traveled with Lionel Hampton's band. At age fifteen, he'd shown Hampton a suite he'd written and been invited to join the band then, but Gladys Hampton had insisted he finish high school first. On graduating from high school, Jones had decided to get as much musical training as he could and had gone instead to the Berklee College of Music in Boston. After that, he went to New York, where Dinah befriended him and gave him his first opportunities as an arranger. On March 15 and 17, 1955, in New York, Dinah recorded eleven songs arranged by Jones: "I Could Write a Book," "Make the Man Love Me," "Blue Gardenia," "You Don't Know What Love Is," "My Old Flame," "Easy Living," "I Get a Kick Out of You," "This Can't Be Love," "A Cottage for Sale," "I Diddle," and "If I Had You." She was accompanied by Clark Terry on trumpet, Jimmy Cleveland on trombone, Paul Quinichette on tenor sax, Cecil Payne on baritone sax, Wynton Kelly (who'd been discharged from the army) on piano, Barry Galbraith on guitar, Keter Betts on bass, and Jimmy Cobb on drums. It was among her most successful recording sessions, packed with talent and "good vibes."

By 1956, Quincy Jones had joined Lionel Hampton's band at last; he went on an international tour with the band

in 1957 and remained in Europe for further study when the
band went home. He would do more work with Dinah on
his return to the United States.

In 1956, Dinah moved into the new Bowery Bank building at 345 West 145th Street, corner of Saint Nicholas
Avenue. The Harlem branch of the bank was located on the
street level, and the top floors were apartments. "We were
on the top floor, the fourteenth floor," recalls LaRue Manns,
who still lives in the building. "We got here through a
friend of Dinah's, who sort of adopted us as daughters. Her
name was Jenny Lee—we called her Aunt Jenny—and she
owned a restaurant at One Hundred and Thirty-fifth Street
and Seventh Avenue. When the building was just being
started, she put in an application for us. The apartments were
supposed to be for low-income tenants, but she got us in."

Dinah's sons were about eight and nine by then, and
she had decided it was time to make a home for them in
New York. She wanted them to go to school in New York,
and she may have wanted to get them away from her family
in Chicago. With LaRue's help, she got them away quickly
and gave her mother little chance to object.

At the time, LaRue was in Chicago, helping to care for
the children and doing her best to get along with Dinah's
mother. "Her mother was having an affair out there at the
church, and Dinah promised to be the guest singer there,
so she flew in for that. She told me, 'Have the kids packed,
and you packed. I want to bring you to New York. I want
to have the kids in school in September in New York. I'm
not gonna let them go there.' She'd had some disagreement
with her mother. So I had the things packed, and when she
came in after she finished the program, she had the car to
wait and sent the fellow in to get the bags. Her mother was
astonished because she didn't know I had done all that, but
I had done most of it while she was at church, you know.
So we sort of eased out, and that's how we got back to

New York. And I don't think the mother ever forgave me for not telling her—she thought I should tell her everything. But Dinah was my boss—she was the one who was sending me my salary and calling me every day.

"We moved in here July fifteenth and we left on the eighteenth and went to California and stayed until September fourteenth, and then I came back with the kids, got them in school. Dinah was on the road, so I had the decorators come in and do the apartment as she wished." During this time, LaRue rarely traveled with Dinah, although any time one of Dinah's longer engagements coincided with a school holiday, she and the children would join Dinah. She remained in New York with the boys, living in the apartment and acting as surrogate mother, helping them with their homework, attending parents' night at the local public school where they were enrolled, and listening to their problems. "On Sundays, we would all three go to church—Adam Clayton Powell's church," says LaRue. "Then we would go to Jenny Lee's for lunch and then downtown to the movies. First, we'd go to one that the boys picked. The next time we'd go to one that I picked, but it was always one that was suitable for children." Dinah returned to New York as often as possible, but her need to make money kept her on the road more than she liked. That fall, she was on the road from the middle of September until Christmas.

By the mid-1950s, postwar prosperity was bringing major changes to the record business. The 45-rpm disk was taking over from the old 78-rpm kind, and since it was lighter, more durable, and easier to make and distribute, it gave a real boost to the business. More and more people were buying records and record players; every club worthy of the name had a jukebox. There were more independent record companies, thanks to the development of tape recording, which reduced the costs of production, and less segregation in the music business, thanks to the greater availability of records of all kinds to people of all kinds. The success of Dinah's records had opened new performing doors for her. She made her first appearance at the Newport Jazz Festival in the summer of 1955 (the second year of the festival) and now could enjoy more bookings on both coasts. In the fall of that year she spent more than a month on the West Coast, performing and recording. Her recording sessions at that time included several with strings, which, says Bobby Shad, of Mercury, "probably cost the company hundreds of thousands of dollars." But Shad was convinced that Dinah deserved a wider audience than she was getting as an R&B artist. "I wanted to take her out of the R&B field. At that time if you brought a record by a black artist to a pop disk jockey, you were dead. They would refuse to play them. I remember bringing up records, and I would refuse to tell them who [the singer] was. I'd say, 'Just listen to the record.' "

The album produced from these recording sessions, *Look to the Rainbow,* contained nothing but romantic love songs—the title track plus "Smoke Gets in Your Eyes," "More Than You Know," "Make Me a Present of You." It did not sell particularly well when it was first released in 1956, and by 1958 the title had been changed to *Dinah.* Shad tried another album with strings with Dinah in the spring of 1956. Recorded in New York, it featured Julian "Cannonball" Adderley on alto sax and Junior Mance on piano and was arranged and conducted by Hal Mooney. Called *In the Land of Hi-Fi,* it contained such songs as "Let's Do It," "I've Got a Crush on You," and "Our Love Is Here to Stay." But after that, Mercury dispensed with the strings, much to Dinah's dismay. There was nothing she enjoyed more than being backed by a full orchestra, but the market ruled, and she didn't sell with strings.

In between recording sessions on the West Coast in the

fall of 1955, she played the Macombo in Hollywood in early October, devoting part of one evening's performance to helping Maria Cole, wife of her friend and fellow Chicagoan by way of Alabama, Nat King Cole. Maria opened at Ciro's on the Sunset Strip that night, and because Dinah could not attend the opening due to her own performing commitments, she devoted part of her own program to songs that Maria had recently recorded for Kapp Records. Now, Dinah herself was a little too black and earthy to play Ciro's, but she put any thoughts of that aside in order to help the wife of Nat King Cole. During that stay on the West Coast, Dinah also played the Club Alabam with Slappy White and Redd Foxx. It was just about that time that White and Foxx broke up. "Redd decided to go with Dusey Williams," says White. "They were recording a party album, with some of the material he used to do before we got together—his blue jokes. The album caught on, and when it did, it made him a strong single." That left Slappy White to fend for himself, and when she reached California that fall, Dinah saw that he needed some help. "So, Dinah is going up to San Francisco and she says, 'Slappy, look, I've got a new car. Why don't you drive my car up to San Francisco for me?' So I drive up to San Francisco, and that night I go by the Blackhawk Club to see her show."

The small jazz club was not loaded with onstage personnel. The bandleader doubled as the emcee. "The band leader, a guy named Vernon Alley, was a bass player," White recalls, "and he would have to set the bass down, go to the microphone, introduce her, then go all the way back, pick the bass up and then start the introduction. So she said to me, 'Slappy, you bring me on the next show,' and I said okay. So the next show she says, 'I've got my own emcee,' and I brought her on. After that, every night I brought her on.

"Every night at showtime she would be late," White

continues, "and I would have to stay up there until she showed up. Whatever jokes I knew, I would tell, but I wasn't used to working by myself. I was always the straight man. Redd Foxx was the comedian. But I had to stall, and so I'd stand up there and tell whatever jokes I knew. I got so good I stayed there a month. When she left to go to Kansas City, the guy kept me there and brought in Johnny Mathis. He was somebody else that Dinah helped. He was just a young kid, but Dinah could see the talent better than I could. She kept saying to the guy who owned the club, 'Put him on,' and he put him on, and after Dinah left, that was the show, Johnny Mathis and me. Two or three months later Dinah had him singing in some movie. Anyway, I stayed at the club long enough to work up a routine.

"Then I left there and went down to Los Angeles, to a jazz club called the Tiffany. I was still there when Dinah came back through town. She was going back East, and I went with her on tour, and I stayed with Dinah doing a single for a long time. Everywhere she worked, I worked. A guy might not want a comic, but Dinah would say, 'This is my comic, and if you ain't got no comic, you ain't got no singer.' So the guy's got to put me on, and I go out there and do the warm-up for her, I'd do the first twenty minutes and then bring her on."

After a time, White was in demand as a single. Often, he would prove to be so good as Dinah's warm-up comedian that a club manager would ask him to stay on after she left. Dinah never minded his staying, nor his going out on tour with other performers. A few months later, he went on tour with B. B. King, playing the Apollo, the Howard in Washington, the Royal in Baltimore, the Paradise in Detroit, and the Regal in Chicago. "Then after I finished that tour, I picked up with Dinah again. She was great at giving people shots, because I had more chances, boy, I did so much wrong all the time, but I stayed with her anyway."

White's most embarrassing performance with Dinah took place in Chicago in 1957 at Mr. Kelly's, a more high-class club than either of them was accustomed to playing. "I was used to working the jazz joints and doing what they called bebop jokes. Opening night at Mr. Kelly's I'm telling these type of stories, but these society people, they don't want to hear none of that. I ain't getting no laughs, and I've been a riot everywhere else because that's the in thing. But at Mr. Kelly's, after the first show I was so disgusted I left the club and went back to the hotel. I bought a fifth of whiskey and drank half of it, and when the next show came around, I'm laying out on the floor. A friend of mine named Prince Spencer, one of the Four Step Brothers, comes down to see me in the second show and Dinah says, 'I don't know where he is.' He comes by the hotel, and here I am on the floor drunk. I was so disgusted, because my material didn't fit the room. That's why I always say that if Dinah Washington had been like Diahann Carroll or Lena Horne or Pearl Bailey, that type of act, I would have been a big comic, because I would have been able to play that type of room. But I was adjusted to the types of rooms that fit Dinah's crowd, like the Five-Four Ballroom.

"Even at those sophisticated spots, she packed them in, because they had all her records. But they didn't give her the same kind of response. Like, in one of her spots, if she sang 'I Don't Hurt Anymore,' they'd scream, 'Yeah!!!' But in one of those halfway sophisticated spots, she'd sing, 'I Don't Hurt Anymore,' and you don't hear no scream at all. That worked on her mind, too, because she was used to hearing those screams when she got into a certain tune, like 'Cold, Cold Heart' or 'Salty Papa Blues.' She very seldom played those places. Those places were for Lena Horne and Dorothy Dandridge. While Lena was at the Waldorf, Dinah was at Birdland. But Dinah was Queen of the Jukebox, and she was getting grand-theft money, a lot more than they were. And I figure she had more fun than they did."

Lena Horne might be invited to sing at the Waldorf, but she was not allowed to stay there. Dinah didn't usually have that problem. She'd get into town and go to a hotel or private home or boardinghouse where she knew she was welcome. Then she'd make tracks for the best soul-food joint around. Everybody knew her, and she'd crack jokes and enjoy being the center of attention. Her dressing room was like Grand Central Station, with admirers coming and going, the local boosters arriving to show her their wares or take her orders, the gay crowd coming to pay their respects. "Dinah was always right in the heart of it," says White, "and that's why she knew all those musicians so well, because she hung out with them."

Evelyn Parker, who was not a musician but a college student, got to know Dinah because of Dinah's hospitality to musicians. "I was going with a fellow who was a sideman in the Apollo band," says Parker. "His name was Arthur Clark, but they called him Babe Clark because he had several other brothers who were musicians and he was the baby. His brother, Pete Clark, also played in the Apollo band. The band was headed by Reuben Phillips, and some of the other members were Selden Powell, Haywood Henry, Eddie Barefield, and a trumpet player named Jones whom everyone called Jonesie. Either the full band or a group from the band would supplement whatever rhythm section Dinah brought in with her when she played the Apollo, but often she would just use the Apollo band, because they were good. They were first-rate musicians. Practically everyone who was in that band later became famous. Babe played woodwinds—alto, tenor, baritone, flute.

"After every engagement, Dinah would give a party at her apartment for the musicians and some of the other people who were in the show. That's how I met her. I used to go with Arthur to her parties. A few of the other guys would take their wives or their girlfriends, but most of them would go alone.'' Those that went alone were either being loyal to their absent wives or girlfriends or had made a conscious decision not to subject their women to Dinah. To be around Dinah, a woman had to be, as Evelyn Parker puts it, ''fairly secure.''

Parker had lived in Detroit in the late 1940s to early 1950s and she'd seen Dinah perform at the Graystone Ballroom and at the Paradise Theatre. She'd also seen Dinah ''just there'' at the Graystone, backstage to visit fellow performers who were appearing there. She was, in fact, a Dinah Washington fan. ''I was from that age when everybody was into that kind of music, and she was it. She was our Aretha Franklin. In the late forties/early fifties there were a lot of small black clubs in Detroit, and they were satisfied to play those places because people gave a lot back to them in terms of appreciation. I also read about her in *Jet* magazine, which followed her better than even the black newspapers. We followed all of that [about Dinah's men and occasional fights], but most people didn't believe too much of it. We just bought records and listened.''

Thus, Evelyn Parker was looking forward to meeting Dinah Washington in the flesh and felt special actually to be going to a party at her apartment. ''The first time I went there, Babe took me there. When I came in the door, she said, 'What you bringin' this simple little dumb bitch in here for?' When he got ready to introduce me, this is what she said. So I just looked at her and didn't say anything, went over to the bar, got a drink, sat down, and, you know, it just went on from there. After that, whenever she would see me, she would laugh and say, 'Oh, there she is again.' I knew it didn't mean anything.''

Parker went to many parties at Dinah's apartment, and on occasion helped Dinah prepare for a party, once bringing along her friend, Lottie Nickens, with whom she was staying

while attending college. She explains that Dinah's apartment
required some setting up for a party. "The windows were
on the Saint Nicholas Avenue side. The living room was
about twelve by twenty-five or twenty-seven, and as you
entered, there was a foyer. The organ was there. The foyer
and the living room merged into one. The kitchen was small,
long, and narrow. People didn't eat in the kitchen—they
ate in the living room. The stuff was set up out there,
including the liquor—it wasn't like a bar that people have
specially built. Her apartment didn't have that kind of room.
The liquor was set out for the party. Sometimes the food
was set out there, too, and sometimes it was served from
the kitchen. She cooked, and LaRue would cook, and the
fellows really appreciated it. They would love to go to
Dinah's house because she would cook, and the party would
go on and on and on. The drinks were plentiful, as much
as you wanted, and they never ran out. People had a good
time. Sometimes there would be brief arguments, usually
occasioned by something that had happened when she was
onstage during the show—somebody messed up or
something—but it would be over in a flash. They all knew
each other and were in the business together. Nobody left
mad. They'd stay on and on and on, and it would be one
big, long party, and it would always end up with her playing
the organ and singing. She would sound, to me, better
sometimes than the pianist she had playing with her. I sometimes wondered why she didn't play more herself, but I
guess she wanted to concentrate on what she was doing,
and that was singing. But at these parties, she was comfortable and relaxed and enjoyed playing."

Dinah was always more comfortable with down-to-earth
people—real people. These included musicians, gays, pimps,
gamblers, and the "little people" who made their living
shining shoes and waiting tables and carrying suitcases and
doing all the myriad menial jobs in society. Patti Austin

spent a considerable amount of time with her during the early years of their relationship. "She was good to 'little people.' But for the grace of God, she could have been one of those 'little people.' She was very warm and wonderful. Instead of a five-dollar tip, she'd give a ten-dollar tip, and then absolutely gloat over the thank-yous. The more thank-yous she got, the higher the head went and the bigger the bust became and the farther back the shoulders would fly: 'Well, of course, it's me, the Queen of the Blues. I just gave you some money. Kiss my ring.' I do remember her having celebrities around and her feeling very shy and out of place. A lot of big white folks, as we say, adored her, and they would come backstage to see her, and she would get so bashful. Kind of look down at the floor and shuffle her feet around and get very demure. And then they'd leave, and she'd mutter something like 'motherfucker.' I remember that she was constantly holding court. She would have an entourage, for days. They usually included a lot of gay people. Because of Dinah, I had my introduction to gay people, though I didn't understand what that meant at the time; I just knew that these guys were kind of 'sweet.' In retrospect, I knew that they were hairdressers and makeup people and dress designers and choreographers. They were working with her, but they hung with her socially as well. She would finish a show and they would go out and hang together. She was idolized by the gay community at that time, particularly the black gay community, and she worked 'em hard—they were gofers for her. Once in a while she would get tired, and then LaRue would have to step in and kind of fend them off. Because it was always, 'Listen to my song, look at this dress I made for you,' everybody wanting to get to her in some way because hopefully she would recognize their talent and help them make it big. What they didn't understand, what most people don't understand, is that usually you're having a tough enough time

just trying to help yourself, which is why Dinah helping me
was a very amazing thing, and something she did not have
to do.''

Dinah had wanted a daughter. Patti became her surrogate
daughter, as well as her protégé. Patti wanted to establish
the basis of the relationship—Dinah was her godmother,
but she didn't think she should call her mother, and Godmother Dinah was a mouthful. ''I said to her, 'What should
I call you, can I call you Aunt Dinah?' She said to me,
'That sounds like some pancakes! Don't be callin' me no
Aunt Dinah, Lord have mercy! Just call me Dinah, please!'
She just kind of cringed, you know. At that time, I didn't
see the essence of that at all. Now that I'm about the same
age as she was at that time, I see *great* humor in that remark
and understand it one hundred percent. But then I didn't
get the joke at all, and I was rather indignant about it: 'Okay,
if you don't like it, excuse me.' I called her Dinah.''

After Dinah befriended and helped Patti, a lot of people
started bringing their talented children around. ''I remember
being there and her saying, 'That ain't gonna get it,' and
of course waving me in front of their faces like a flag. She
was always doing that; I made a lot of enemies thanks to
her. She loved to do that. And I remember that her relatives,
her family, copped a big attitude about me: 'Who's this
kid? What're you doing everything for this kid for? She's
not your blood.' I'm talking about her sisters, her mother
maybe—I remember it only vaguely.''

LaRue Manns concurs. ''Dinah used to spend a lot of
nice money on Patti. Anything she saw, she didn't care
what it cost, because Patti deserved it. And she just loved
Patti, and Patti and her family loved Dinah. Dinah's family,
her sisters, and all, would say, 'She's buying that for Patti,
ought to be buying it for me.' Her mother didn't want Dinah
spending any money anywhere but for them. They had a
little jealousy for Patti, and of course a little jealousy for

me, and a lot of things went down and were said, and Dinah was hassled. But, time changes, you know.''

The boys were the only family members who did not resent Patti. She says, ''They didn't have a sister, and they used to treat me like the queen bee; and I was always terribly prissy, with my little white gloves and crinolines, and I was working the room to death when I was with those two. They ate it up, and they were very protective and very sweet to me all the time. I didn't see them that often—she was always on the road, and they never came to visit me—so I was rent-a-sister for a little while every now and then. She'd come home for a week or so and ask my parents if I could stay the weekend with her, and they'd ask me if I wanted to, and I always said yes. She wanted the boys to be around me because she thought I would be a good influence, especially the way I spoke. They had no command of the English language at all, and I remember the first night we went there and had dinner with the whole family. The boys would say, 'Can we have meat 'n' patatas, please?' I mean, we're talking real down-home brothers. The boys could hardly form a sentence—no articulation at all—and she was totally disillusioned by that. Around then I was spending a lot of time with Ray Robinson's wife, Edna, because she and my mother were very good friends. Edna was terribly educated and articulate, and she enunciated e-ver-y syllable. I adored this woman—thought she was the most fabulous woman I'd ever seen—and I was absorbing her way of speaking. Dinah didn't know where I was getting it from, but she liked what she heard. She'd say to the boys, 'Just listen to that, just listen.' They never showed any animosity. If anything, they were curious. They'd say, 'Oh, yeah? Das how I'm 'sposed to talk? Do that again.' They'd kind of crane their necks a little more and say, 'Oh, okay, if that's what you want, I'll try to do it.' I could do no wrong over there, which was not a bad deal.''

Gordon Austin recalls, "Dinah was very disappointed in the boys' education. She used to say, 'Jesus Christ, they're so dumb.' She was angry, really deeply angry about this. I don't know if she blamed herself or not, but she was really upset, because she knew how hard it was out there. 'I don't want no dummies in my family,' she'd say. The more she talked about it, the more she got worked up. She had some education, but she knew that it took more than she had and that she was lucky that she had a gift that would carry her through life."

LaRue, who had chief responsibility for the day-to-day well-being of the children at that time, was also worried about the two little boys in sixty-five-dollar sweaters and diamond cufflinks who couldn't read or write. "The teacher was saying that one of them was a little slow in this, the other a little slow in that. I had to start reaching out for special schools for them. I found one, and they went there for a while, but then I found out it was a school for semi-retarded kids. They found out, too, and said they didn't want to go. They went to the Professional Children's School for a while. Finally we got them in a private school, a military school upstate, and she began to be satisfied with their progress and their grades."

The boys came home during school vacations and at holidays and so were not separated from Dinah much more than they had been when they were living in the apartment in the Bowery Bank building and going to school in the city.

About the time the boys went away to school, Ferris Kimbrough, Dinah's young stepsister, joined Dinah in New York. She was twenty by then and eager to see the world, a chance she had with a famous aunt. Dinah had made a point of paying as much attention as she could to her young stepsisters and stepbrothers, who had a hard time getting along in school because of their famous stepsister. "People expected us to wear designer clothes and have great voices," says Kimbrough. "One of the most embarrassing things happened my senior year. We were going to have a talent show, and everybody, even one of the teachers, said, 'Well, if Dinah Washington is really your sister, why don't you get her to come to the talent show?' So I asked her to come, and she did. She showed up with her whole band. But they wouldn't let her go on. It was a high school talent show, and professionals weren't allowed—the union wouldn't allow it. She was very upset. Of course nobody had really expected her to come, and when she did, they wouldn't let her on."

Ferris joined Dinah in New York after graduation. With the boys away at school, there was usually enough room, although as Ferris recalls, the existence or nonexistence of a spare bed didn't stop a lot of people from sleeping there anyway. "They were sleeping on the hard floor, without even mattresses. You would never believe this, it being New York and all, but Dinah's door was almost never locked. People didn't have money, didn't have jobs, and Dinah would say, 'Look, my house is full, people are sleeping on the floor, but if you want to come to my house, there's always enough food, you can always have something to eat.' And as soon as they would get full, or she would get them a job, or give them some money, they would do something to her. They'd steal something from her—a diamond, a mink coat, a TV. I was there the day somebody stole the TV and the mink coat. One of her friends came in and asked me for something, distracted my attention. I went out with that person, and the other person came in and took the stuff out. And these were *friends* of hers! And the thing was, she wouldn't take this out on the people who did it to her, she took it out on everybody else. I don't know why."

One by one, all three members of Dinah's backup trio left that year. Wynton Kelly went first, Keter Betts soon afterward. "We had one heck of a thing, and she fired me," says Betts. "In fact, I think when she gave me the notice, she was crying. It was an accumulation of things, not personality differences so much as a part of everybody's growing up. It got to be hard, all that traveling, all that driving, doing that and playing, doing what we called hit and run. Like, if we're in Philadelphia and we're going to play Washington the next night, and then go on to Cleveland, Washington would be the hit and run. We'd come in there and play and then take on out to Cleveland, driving all night, behind the wheel for twelve or thirteen hours. Phew!

"I got off the road and started a whole other thing around Washington. Then I hooked up with Charlie Bird and then I've been with Ella [Fitzgerald] on and off since '64."

Finally, Jimmy Cobb left. "I stayed in New York and gigged around New York, and then I went with Cannonball Adderley, Sam Jones. Then I went with Dizzy Gillespie and later Miles Davis, and then Wynton Kelly and Paul Chambers and myself had a trio for about five years. [Kelly died in Toronto in 1970.] Dinah and I would see each other now and then. When she moved into the Bowery Bank Building, she'd have parties, and I'd sometimes go there, but I got the feeling she was trying to use me. I'd go to see her perform. She used to call me Abe Lincoln, because I had a beard, and I'd be out there, and someone would tell her I was in the audience, and she'd say some things that would make the girl I was with mad."

Around Christmas 1956, LaRue Manns, one of the people on whom Dinah had been in the habit of taking out her pain for nearly ten years, actually decided that she'd had enough and left. "We were in Kansas City, and we were all at this hotel. I thought Dinah was in for the night, but some of the musicians came by and said she was down the hall with some other guys playing Tonk, which was a card game. They told me she'd gotten out of bed and put on her

robe and gone down the hall to play Tonk. So I go out with
some of the guys to a restaurant, and I forget that I still
have my jewelry on, a ring and a necklace. Meanwhile,
Dinah goes to my room and doesn't see me. She knows it's
a new town and I've got all my jewelry on. So she wraps
her mink coat around her and goes out looking for me.
We're on our way back when we meet her in the street.
She screams at me in the middle of the street: Why didn't
I tell her? I told her I was grown, I didn't always have to
tell her where I was going. The guys who were with me
tried to explain, but she got mad and cussed them out,
talking about if they didn't stay out of it, they'd get fired.
We got back to the hotel, and it was one of those times
[when I'd just had enough]. It was near Christmastime, and
I was tired, weary. I had taken a lot of harsh things from
time to time, but I'd overlooked them because I knew it
didn't mean anything. But sometimes, you know, even iron
wears out. I told her, 'Rather than have arguments like this,
I'd better just go. I would like to have all the money and
jewelry that belongs to me (she kept it in a strongbox and
also had the key) and I'm leaving, going home.' She says,
'Good.' She gets everything, lays it on the bed. She doesn't
think I'm really leaving. I call one of the guys and ask him
to take me to the train station. I get on the train. Before I
got home—the train took twelve to fourteen hours—she
had called my mother, crying. 'Please talk to her,' she said
to my mother, 'and have her call me as soon as she arrives,
'cause I want to know that she's okay.' I did call her when
I got ready. She boohooed and cried. She called her mother
in Chicago, and her mother called my mother. Oh, it was
such a mess! So I told her that I was going to stay home
for the holiday, which was about four days. Then I would
meet her back in New York. We got everything straightened
out, and we didn't have any more problems from then on.''

Dinah had a way of presuming that she owned people,

and even those who loved her most had to remind her, from time to time, that she didn't own them, in spite of how much she had done for them. "She had a heart like the Grand Canyon," says Patti Austin. "I'm sure she would have helped everybody who crossed her path, because that was just her nature. But at the same time, if they did *anything* to piss her off, that was it—'Give me that suit, give me those cufflinks, give me my shoes, give me my hat, get off my stage.' With acceptance of her kindness came that debt, and I think probably I was one of the few people in her life that she never did that to. With me, she was totally selfless—I love you, this is for you, you're good, you're talented. She loved talented people." Patti Austin's advantage was that she was not only talented but much too young to be any kind of threat.

Dinah Washington,
Queen of the Blues, in the late 1940s

Even offstage,
Dinah was a fussy dresser.

Patti Austin appeared with Dinah.
Wynton Kelly is on the piano.

Dinah in 1963

Dinah (third from left) weds Eddie Chamblee on the stage of the Royal Casino, Washington, D.C. To her right are LaRue Manns and Dinah's agent. To her left are Eddie Chamblee and Slappy White. Patti Austin is the flower girl.

Dinah never forgot she had
once been so poor she had had to share a pair
of stockings with her mother.

Dinah in 1957 with chocolates containing slivers of glass that had been sent to her through the mail.

Ann Little's birthday celebration in the ballroom of the Hotel Teresa in Harlem. From left, Dizzy Gillespie (wearing glasses), Quincy Jones (holding bottle), LaRue Manns, Dinah. At the back, next to the wall lamp, is Jimmy Cobb.

Dinah in performance

Wilt "The Stilt" Chamberlain hoists a surprised Dinah
to face her husband-to-be Dick "Night Train" Lane in
June 1963 when Dinah was appearing at Wilt's
Venice West nightclub.

Dick "Night Train" Lane
of the Detroit Lions football
team became Dinah's seventh
husband in July 1963.

Dinah's casket is maneuvered
through the crowds to the hearse at
St. Luke's Baptist Church, Chicago,
in December 1963.

Of Men and Music

FERRIS Kimbrough realized soon after she went to stay with Dinah that it was in her best interest not to be too conspicuous when other people were around. "I had a great shape, but no talent; she had a great talent, but no shape. To me, that should have been her least worry, but she worried about it all the time. Whenever we would go to work, I would wear pants and sweaters and try to keep a low profile, knowing how she was. But there was this time when we were in Florida and it was very hot. She was singing at a very nice country club, and I decided to get dressed and go out. She had given me a gorgeous black dress, and I put it on and went to see her show. Most of the time I stayed backstage when she was performing, but sometimes I went out in front, and she'd ask me how she'd done. This time, there was some trouble. One of the fellows in the band had missed a note, and she was getting on him, and then she looked around to see what had happened, and she saw me standing there in this dress. 'Go take my dress off!' she yelled. Knowing her, I didn't pay her any mind. She was always doing that, picking a fight with somebody. She'd pick a fight with a waitress and get her fired and then come home and cry about it."

Ferris Kimbrough says that when she met Dinah, around 1953, Dinah was a size twenty-two and waging a constant battle with her weight. While Kimbrough, among others, believes that Dinah hated being fat because she felt it made her less attractive, young Patti Austin does not feel that Dinah's ego suffered because she was overweight. There is no question, however, that all that weight did affect her stamina on the road. Ironically, being on the road so much caused her to gain weight and at the same time militated against weight gain. Gordon Austin explains: "It was awfully hard to travel and do all those one-nighters and have a proper diet. Being black didn't help, because a lot of times you couldn't get decent food. You'd have to go to the supermarket or some convenience store and buy bologna and bread and eat it in the car just to keep from having any kind of hassle. And when you did find a place where you could sit down and eat, it was all that soul food that you'd gorge on. Dinah was a southern gal, and she loved ham hocks and blackeye peas, spareribs and potato salad, yams, all that fattening stuff. She'd try to avoid it, but when you were on the road, you needed something. Everybody needed something—what it was depended on the kind of person you were. The exhaustion, the tension, you couldn't let it get to you when you were performing. Onstage, you'd perform as if nothing was wrong. But then you'd finish and you'd sit down and let go. You had to blow to get some of the tension out. Some guys would get drunk, some would smoke pot, the overweight ones would indulge in food, just eat, eat, eat, to cover up all that emotion. But you couldn't eat, eat, eat and have the stamina to continue on the road. Dinah knew she couldn't keep eating and do what she was doing all the time."

LaRue Manns remembers that Dinah first sought chemical help for her weight problem after she saw how much weight bandleader Paul Whiteman had lost. "I think he was

booked by the same agency—Joe Glaser's agency—and
they would see each other quite often. He had been a heavy
man, and when she saw how much weight he had lost, she
asked him about it. He told her about this doctor that, at
the time, was on West 52nd or West 56th Street, Dr. Harry
K. Stone. So, she went to this doctor and she got tuned into
pills, and pretty soon she had a pill for everything.'' The
pills did help her take off weight, but from that time on her
weight varied greatly, depending on her own body chemistry
and how it reacted with the pills. ''She was up and down,''
says Gordon Austin. ''She would come and go,'' says Jimmy
Cobb.

Recalls LaRue Manns, ''A lot of people thought she
was on street stuff, but it was all prescription, all legit. If
she wanted to stay up late hours, to record or something,
she had a pill for that. Then when she got ready to go to
bed or relax, she would take sleeping pills. Those came in
two sizes, and sometimes she would take two. On a few
occasions, she would be depressed or something, she'd be
upset because she was tired and couldn't rest like everybody
else, and she'd be walking through the apartment and she'd
take too many. I'd have to walk her and pour black coffee
down her and walk her and walk her and keep her together
and call the doctor. That happened once in a while.''

Most of the time, however, Dinah handled the pills, and
the booze, and the work, and the responsibilities. She tried
to have at least a few people she loved around her at all
times, and in early 1957, after some seven years out of legal
wedlock, she had a husband again. His name was Eddie
Chamblee, and naturally he was a musician, a sax player.
He and Dinah had known each other in high school but had
not kept in touch after his graduation in 1940. Eddie had
gone into the army, and Evelyn Parker knew him then. ''I
was in school at Talladega [Alabama], and he was stationed
at the army post near there,'' Parker recalls. He played in

a band at the post, and they used to play every weekend
for dances. My girlfriend, Laretha Black, was Eddie's girlfriend, and I was [drummer] Chico Hamilton's girlfriend.
We called ourselves that, but we really weren't. Our campus
had been depleted of men by the draft.''

After he got out of the army, Chamblee played with any
number of bands that were on the same circuit as Dinah,
but it was in late 1955/early 1956, when Chamblee was
with Lionel Hampton's band, that they first got interested
in each other. Then the Hampton band went to Europe (the
same European tour that Quincy Jones was on). ''But we
kept in touch,'' says Chamblee. ''We wrote letters.'' Chamblee, who was on his second marriage, was also in the
process of his second divorce by the time the Hampton band
returned to the United States. According to Patti Austin,
Dinah probably helped the divorce along. ''She was a talent
f-----,'' says Austin. ''She also had a big ego. She wanted
to make a man a star. She also loved to marry somebody
else's husband. She bought a lot of divorces and paid for
more child support than anybody can think of. It was a great
challenge to take somebody else's man. There was a lot
about Dinah that was very butch; there was a lot in her that
was masculine in that she liked the challenge of fighting for
some stuff. That's kind of a southern-woman thing; southern
women will get down on the ground and fight over some
sucker, in a minute—that's my man. She had that in her
blood, and she would do it.''

Years later, in one of her bitter moods, Dinah claimed
that when Eddie joined her, ''he was living at the Alvin
Hotel in New York, broke and disgusted. I loved him, so
I lent him money to straighten himself out. To be near him,
we booked his band with me as an act, and we traveled the
country together.'' In Chamblee's recollection, he joined
Dinah's entourage as a single. ''She was traveling with a
trio—piano, bass, trumpet. I was the odd man out.'' He

was "in" in the romance department, however, and after two or three months Dinah proposed to him. "It wasn't that strange," says Chamblee. "She just said, 'Let's get married,' and we'd kind of gotten together anyhow, so she was just the one who first said it."

Chamblee told Leslie Gourse, author of *Louis' Children*, "I had no idea I would marry Dinah. . . . You've got to lay it on charisma. People fell in love with Dinah's voice. And she had her womanly wiles. She was warm and kind to me. I respected her musicianship, and I had nobody. I was just divorced at the time. She showed an interest in me. Under certain circumstances she was a beautiful woman. And on stage, emoting, she could tear your heart out."

They were married in Washington, D.C., on March 6, 1957, on the stage of the Royal Casino. "At one time they didn't allow blacks in there," says LaRue Manns, "and this was the opening up. I think she was among the first black stars to appear there, and she was married on the stage to let people know." LaRue, wearing a dress of the same material as Dinah's, was maid of honor, Patti Austin the flower girl, Slappy White the best man. White nearly missed the wedding, having been assigned various errands beforehand, and several states away. Less than a week before the wedding, Dinah and her entourage had been playing gigs in Florida, finishing in Miami. "She has to leave to go up to Washington, D.C.," says White, "and she says, 'Slappy, you bring the car up.' I say, 'Okay,' and I'm not realizing how soon I'm supposed to be up there. She's playing at a club in Washington in a couple of days, but I wasn't going to work that gig. I'm not going to work until the next week, when she's going to do Baltimore, my hometown. So I'm in no hurry to get back, and I'm at the racetrack having a good time, when I find out that the piano player called. All Dinah's music is in the trunk of the car, and she can't open without it. This is Sunday, and she's supposed to open on

Tuesday. So, I get on the road and I'm flying. Somewhere in Georgia I get a ticket; the policeman says I was doing seventy-six miles per hour. After that, I'm flying again. In North Carolina I get another ticket. The policeman says I'm doing seventy-six miles per hour. I get two tickets for doing seventy-six miles per hour. I keep going. I take No-Doz. I drive this car night and day and I get there and rehearsal is at two o'clock, and I get into town three hours early. I pull up across from where Dinah is staying and I go into the house and I say, 'Dinah, guess what? I got two tickets for doing seventy-six miles per hour. Here, put this ten dollars on the number two hundred and seventy-six.' So they go to the rehearsal, and I go to sleep. When I wake up, Dinah has a bag full of money for me—this is numbers money, so you get paid off in twenties, you get six to one—and she's saying, 'Goddamn, why didn't I play that number?'

"The next day, she's going to get married to Eddie Chamblee. I go down and serve as best man, but I'm not thinking about that. I'm thinking about going home to Baltimore with all this money, I can give all my people some money, all my sisters and brothers, and be the big-time celebrity coming home.''

Dinah's schedule permitted no honeymoon for herself and her new husband. Less than a week after their wedding they were in Los Angeles, playing at Zardi's, a jazz club on Hollywood and Vine. A box of candy arrived for Dinah in care of the club. A typewritten note inside read, ''My tail is short as you can see, goodbye to you from me.'' It was signed ''Yasha.'' Dinah didn't know what it meant and didn't pay much attention to it. She was always getting candy and flowers and other gifts. She passed the box around, but apparently no one ate any of the candy. Eddie Chamblee was later quoted as saying, ''For some reason I didn't like the way it looked, so I didn't take a piece.'' Says Slappy

White, "I was always in her dressing room, and if I'd been there, I would have taken a piece, but for some reason I didn't go to her room that day." Dinah gave the box of candy to a friend, Mrs. Ann Moore, who bit into a piece and discovered a quarter-inch sliver of glass in it. She called the police. On inspection, all the pieces of candy were laced with glass. To this day, no one except the sender knows who sent the candy or why. There was speculation that it had been sent by an old boyfriend of Dinah's or an old girlfriend of Eddie's, but nothing more than speculation ever came out of the police investigation. Patti Austin remembers being shocked when she heard of the incident and later hearing talk that the candy had been sent by some woman who'd been jilted for Dinah.

Patti remembers another unpleasant surprise that Dinah got in the mail. "Billy Eckstine sent her a box of chitlins one time. They had a serious feud going, and he sent her some chitlins in the mail, slow postage, so that by the time they arrived, they would be green and you could smell them a mile away. Typical bebop sense of humor. Bebop musicians loved to play practical jokes and tell jokes. There's a classic tale of Dinah getting on the wrong bus. This sounds like a typical bebop joke, but knowing Dinah, it could have happened. She was on a tour, and they were traveling by bus, and they all stopped somewhere, and she got onto this bus that was full of mental patients. The attendant was counting patients before the bus pulled out and he kept getting one too many. So he counts again, one, two, three, four, five, and he gets to Dinah, and he says, 'Who are you?' She says, 'I'm Queen of the Blues.' He says, 'Yep, you definitely belong here. Six, seven, eight, nine, ten, eleven—' We don't know if that's true or not, but I hope it is."

Things like that were always happening to Dinah. She was always hitting somebody over the head with his instrument, or being hit over the head, or throwing a glass at some woman, or being sued by some woman. Ferris Kimbrough recalls that she traveled everywhere with Dinah during the time she was with her—Miami, Fort Lauderdale, Tampa, Jacksonville, Philadelphia, Chicago—except Saint Louis. "In Saint Louis, she had to travel light, get in and get out quick, because there was a woman in Saint Louis who had a grudge against her and who, anytime she saw that Dinah was playing someplace, would run in and slap a lawsuit on her." She was known to have walked out on engagements, though according to her musicians she usually had a reason. She also wouldn't take any lip from her audiences. Jack Wilson believes that her reputation for being "bombastic" is what kept her out of the high-class clubs. "They were scared to take a chance on her because of her legendary temper." Still, if Dinah had not had such a volatile personality, one wonders if she would have been able to invest her songs with so much emotion, and that was a quality that everyone who ever played with her or saw her perform or listened to her records, remarked on, over and over.

"Dinah had a group of conflicting emotions that had the most to do with how she presented her songs," says Eddie Chamblee. "She sang a ballad better sometimes if she was hurt. Not necessarily by a man, but maybe because of her sons or her mother. . . . Dinah was like Judy Garland. She drew all the whores and pimps and losers. Certain entertainers draw a certain element in audiences and in friends. If a singer sings a loser's love song, the audience identifies. 'Somewhere Over the Rainbow' is a loser's lament. 'Blue Skies' is another. 'Look to the Rainbow' is still another. Dinah sang those. 'I'll win somewhere,' she sang. Dinah figured that somewhere over the rainbow she would find a man who loved her. She sang songs of losers."

Dinah used to say that she never sang a song that she

couldn't feel and make her own. "Getting inside a tune is so important," she told Jack Maher of *Metronome* in April 1957, "and when you do there's a feeling—a strong feeling—that comes out. When you get inside of a tune the soul in you should come out. You should just be able to step back and let that soul come right out. It should flow out of you. That's what I feel I do. That's what I want and try to do."

She did not believe that this quality of soulfulness in her singing should pigeonhole her as a blues singer. "You know who my favorite singers are today, really the top two?" she asked Maher. "Frank Sinatra and Nat King Cole. They get inside of a tune and yet no one calls them blues singers. Frank and Nat use words and tunes so wonderfully that they make you know what they mean." But by that time Dinah had been called Queen of the Blues so long that she could not shake the label. She knew it meant that her records were always assigned to the R&B charts, were not as readily available in white neighborhoods as in black, were not played on white radio stations nearly as often as on black stations. She would like to have broken out of those strictures, as Nat King Cole had managed to do. A couple of decades later, she might not have felt the need to distance herself from a label that was so identifiably black, but in the late 1950s blues meant black music, and black music did not have the same lucrative market as did white music.

By 1957 that "white" music included rock 'n' roll, a style unabashedly influenced by black rhythm and blues but so changed, in Dinah's opinion, by singers like Elvis Presley, who did "fieldwork" at the Apollo, that it was hardly music at all. "It's based on the blues and jazz, but Elvis Presley has done something to it," she said in March 1957. "The big audience for it is kids, and when they grow enough to understand what it is, they won't like it. But to them it's like the Susie-Q used to be: something to make their mothers mad. It'll die out; after a while even the FBI won't be able to find Elvis Presley.'' Dinah was not alone in her short-sightedness. Her heroes, Nat King Cole and Frank Sinatra, shared her distaste for rock 'n' roll. Cole often included in his performances of that time a novelty tune called "Mr. Cole Won't Rock 'n' Roll.'' Sinatra militated against the music, calling it subversive and a danger to the morals of American youth.

By the middle 1950s, television had become an impor-tant venue for marketing musical talent, but that rarely in-cluded black musical talent. For all his crossover record sales, even Nat King Cole couldn't stay on the tube for a half hour weekly. The problem was sponsorship and the fear of advertisers that their products would be hurt by association with black performers. The old bugaboo of southern audiences kept Cole off even local New York sta-tions, though how the advertisers who were approached to sponsor the show could insist that they feared offending listeners who would never, in actuality, see the show is difficult to understand. Dinah was much less acceptable to white audiences than Cole, and her TV appearances were limited chiefly to local broadcasts. Her first major television appearance was with Rex Harrison on a CBS-TV *Du Pont Show of the Month* in 1957. Dinah hardly set the show on fire. Nor did she enjoy the experience. "I had to stand on a white line all day, and then on the day of the show I just had to sit waiting. That's not for me,'' she told a Toronto interviewer a couple of years later. Local shows? "They're okay. I just come in and sing or mouth a song and go home.'' She was convinced that the lack of spontaneity was the reason why most network television jazz shows didn't make it. In the years since recording the skeptical novelty tune "TV Is the Thing (This Year),'' Dinah had become an avid TV watcher. She confessed that she turned her set on as soon as she woke up and watched whenever she could. But she preferred dramatic series like *The Rifleman*, *Wyatt Earp*, *Peter Gunn*, and *M-Squad*. She steered clear of watching music and variety shows unless they featured Cole or Sinatra.

Call her shortsighted or insufficiently commercial-minded—Dinah never forsook the way she sang, and her real fans have been grateful to her ever since. Call it soul, call it blues, call it whatever, there was nothing like it to touch the heart of even the most hardened individual. Says Charles Davis, "I never experienced anything with a vocalist that could make a whole band cry. That happened quite frequently."

Davis, a baritone sax player who joined Dinah in 1957, shared Chicago roots with Dinah and had gone to the same high school there, Wendell Phillips High. "We had one of the same band directors," says Davis, "Walter Henry Dyett. Wendell Phillips burned down, I think, and I also attended DuSable while they rebuilt it. I didn't know her when I was growing up, I was younger than she."

By 1957, Dinah was traveling most of the time with a seven-piece band led involuntarily by Eddie Chamblee. Chamblee attributes their getting along well, at least in the early period of their relationship, to the fact that "I've always been a follower, so no problems. She was the star." After their marriage, Dinah wanted him to be her bandleader. "She wanted me to be out front as the bandleader, and I didn't really like that. I tried it for a while, to please her, but I'm happier in the background." Dinah also had Eddie sing duets with her onstage. The critic for *Variety*, reviewing her show at Chicago's Black Orchid in April 1958, called the duets "moderately charming" but said they "failed to register as a high point." All the other musicians knew that he was the leader because he was Dinah's husband, but that didn't particularly bother them. They were paid well—exceptionally well for the time, according to Charles Davis: "She always appreciated musicians."

To a man, and the occasional woman piano player, they loved her. They knew that she recognized and supported talent and that she was a consummate professional when it came to her music. "She had flawless pitch, excellent diction," says Jack Wilson, who played with her for a total of about two years. "Dinah could be out cursing and misusing and breaking verbs and everything like that, but when she got on the stage, her pronunciation and her enunciation were letter-perfect. She never mispronounced a word, as I've heard Sarah Vaughan do; or as I've heard Ella Fitzgerald do. She always pronounced with almost alarming clarity. And she could handle any kind of material—standards, blues. She could even take a nothing tune and make something out of it. She could touch everybody because she was such an emotional singer, and I think that what struck me most was that she was a good piano player, too. Dinah played the shit out of the piano. When I first joined her, I used to make a mistake and she'd come and sit down on the piano bench and keep scooting over until she'd moved me off the bench so she could play herself. I don't know why she didn't play onstage or on recordings herself, but I do know that she didn't really consider herself a piano player, and she had the greatest piano players with her."

Charles Davis also recalls that Dinah was no slouch on musical instruments. "She played piano and organ, a little bass fiddle. She and Sarah Vaughan would jam sometimes—various places they'd meet up on the road and have little jam sessions, and I remember they did that in Birdland once."

In retrospect, these musicians realize that she taught them all they needed to know to go out and work with anyone after working with her. Jack Wilson is particularly grateful to her, because he was a young unknown when she

took him on. "I was in Atlantic City. I had gone there for
the beginning of the summer season on the pretext of getting
a job with a band that was later to be called the American
Jazz Quartet. This was just a bunch of local cats—Peppy
Hennett from Baltimore, Calvin Risley from Newark, Jeffrey Wilkes also from Newark (he was a saxophone player
in Count Basie's band). So, we went there for a gig, but
there was no gig. We were trying to hang on there because
we knew the season was going to start, and we went around
to a place called the Cotton Club, a jazz place, and took a
job at no salary, just "playing for the door." Well, there
wasn't nobody in Atlantic City before the season started—
a lot of nights you could be playing in there and you could
fire a shot in there and not hit nobody. There was nobody
in there but the bartender, and he was drugged. Finally, the
season started up, and the first person they had in there was
Miles [Davis], and we worked opposite Miles, and the thing
started to be pretty good. Dinah was due in next—Dinah
and the Bud Powell Trio and the Finnias Newborne Quartet.

"So, what happened was, Bud Powell got drunk. Dinah's piano player took Bud out and got him drunk before
the show. Bud goes on, and when he takes his bow, he falls
off the stage and wipes out the whole first row of tables.
They said, 'The amazing Bud Powell,' and he stood up
from the piano and took a bow and kept on going. Dinah
is upset with her piano player and she fires him on the spot.
Now she needs a piano player.

"I was upstairs in my room over the club. The son of
the owner comes up and says Dinah Washington needs a
piano player. I had to go get a shirt out of the dirty
laundry—it had been in the pile a long time because I didn't
have the money to get it cleaned. I put on this dirty shirt
and my little suit and went downstairs. Dinah looked at me
and I looked at her and she said, 'You're the piano player?'
I said, 'Yes.' She said, 'Okay, you go up and play this next

set.' I was scared to death—we're not just talking scared, we're talking terror. Number one, Dinah had all these complex arrangements by Quincy [Jones] and cats like that. The band was an excellent band. I was worried about reading the music and playing for her, too. Sometimes the rest of the cats laid out and there'd be nobody but me and her. I stayed scared for about three weeks to a month. She used to call me that little no-playing nigger. Years later, I asked Eddie Chamblee, 'Why did you and Dinah keep me with the band?' He said, 'Man, Dinah said the first night you played that you were going to be a motherfucker, but that you just had to get your shit together, and that's why she kept you. Because she thought you could play.' But I'll tell you right now, I was not ready to be with anyone of Dinah's stature. I was just not ready. As a result, we made some beautiful music together and there's a lot of it still left on the records we did together.

"She had a tremendous insight about musicians and cats that would sound good with her and cats she wouldn't sound good with. Around the time I joined her, Miles Davis's album *Miles Ahead* came out. The arranger was Gil Evans [who had also arranged "Birth of the Cool" and whose work with Davis is considered classic]. Naturally, all the musicians were crazy about that record, and me and Johnny Coles asked her why she didn't get Gil Evans to write some arrangements for her. But Dinah said, 'No, I don't think so,' and she said it in such a way that it made us think. She was remarkably intelligent about music. She knew that Gil Evans without Miles Davis wouldn't have produced that music. In effect, she was saying, 'Gil Evans and me ain't gonna work together because I can't tell him what to do like Miles does and I just don't think he is going to go with my thing. But she didn't say that. She just said, 'No, I don't think so.' I had to experience playing some Gil Evans music away from Miles Davis—I was with Gerald Wilson and we were the house band at the Monterey Jazz Festival

and we had to play a Gil Evans arrangement for Helen
Merrill—before I really understood what Dinah was talking
about.''

Not long after Jack Wilson and Charles Davis joined
the band, they went to New York for a major recording
session that produced twenty songs and signaled a stylistic
departure for Dinah. All the songs were Fats Waller's, and
the album was titled, appropriately, *Dinah Sings Fats Waller*.
Later that year, she would record *Dinah Sings Bessie Smith*
in Chicago. "Everybody that was anybody was on this
record date,'' says Wilson, "In the trumpet section was
Charlie Shavers, Clark Terry, Joe Neuman, Ernie Royal,
Emmett Berry, and Johnny Coles (from our band). The
trombones were Jimmy Cleveland, Herbie Green, Tommy
Mitchell, and Julian Priester (from our band). The saxo-
phones were Jerome Richardson, Hal Macusic, Frank West,
and Charles Davis and Eddie Chamblee from our band. The
rhythm section was Richard Evans on bass, myself on piano,
our drummer named Westley Landers, and Freddie Greene
on guitar. The arranger was Ernie Wilkins. [The usual discographies include Doc Severinson on trumpet and a few
other differences in personnel.] And, baby, when I walked
into that record date, I was so knocked off my feet by all
these cats I'd been reading about all my life. A lot of us
guys [in the band] were scared. Some of the guys had some
smoke but we would not go down to the bathroom that was
on the floor, because those other guys were in there smoking
and we didn't want to get a contact high—we were worried
about reading that music. But sure enough, as fate would
have it, the drummer messed up and couldn't play his part.
They took a break for about fifteen minutes and then they
moved our drummer's drums out and moved Charlie Persip's in. Then they kept on stroking. The rest of us guys in
the band had our noses so far into that music you would
have thought something was on it.

"Dinah knew them all on a first-name basis, knew how

they could play and would say, 'I want you to solo on this,'
or whatever. All the musicians liked to work with Dinah
because she gave you such a boost on the stand. I think her
favorite saxophonist was Lucky Thompson—he takes a
beautiful solo on 'Never Let Me Go.' [Actually, this was
in an earlier session.] She had her musical contacts, and her
musicians went all the way back to her days with Lionel
Hampton when Milt Buckner was in the band. She knew
the cats, and they all loved her, and the feeling was mutual.''

Jack Wilson's feeling of love for Dinah just continued
to increase. While they were in New York for that record
date, they were invited to play a set at the Copacabana,
which, says Wilson, ''was probably the biggest club in New
York on the money side at that time.'' Dinah had told her
musicians to gather up all the ''big-band music,'' the arrangements they had been using for the recording sessions,
and they were not worried. But once they got there, they
realized they were going to have to play with the house
band, which, with fifteen pieces, was large for the time.
And for Jack Wilson, there was yet another surprise in store.
''Just before we went on, she said to me, 'Oh, by the way,
you're going to conduct.' I said, 'Wait a minute.' But before
I could say anything else, she was gone. So, I go out there,
and the musicians got the music up, and I tell them what's
going to be next and what we are going to do, and that's
all I remember. I don't remember anything about it. Dinah
said it was a motherfucker of a show, but I don't remember
nothing about it. She said I conducted the band, said I
walked away from conducting the band and even sat down
at the piano and played something at the piano, got back
up, cut the band off and everything. But I was in shock, I
don't remember shit. Of course those cats at the Copa were
all crack musicians. Those cats could read anything you put
in front of them. Good thing, because I was on automatic
pilot the whole time.''

She loved her musicians, and, according to Jack Wilson, didn't want anyone else criticizing them. But fifteen-plus years in show business hadn't given her any more patience with mistakes. She expected a lot from her musicians and was not afraid to correct them on the stage in front of an audience. "I got fired many times onstage," says Charles Davis, "but that was just for the moment, that passed." They had to understand that, and in addition, care about Dinah a whole lot, to take the kind of abuse she could dish out. When guitarist Irving Ashby was a member of Nat King Cole's trio, he worked with Dinah in New York. "She had to go through the band room to get to her dressing room, and after she came off stage, she'd really give it to them—'Hello, motherfucker, how's yo' blackass mother? If she play like you, she ain't shit!' She'd say this to the guys, one by one, as she passed them."

Quite frequently, Dinah's emotional outbursts onstage and off were due not so much to any flaws in her musicians' playing as to other, entirely unrelated things. She was still on the road almost constantly, and being on the road hadn't gotten any easier as the years went on. She had money worries, troubles with Eddie over who was in charge of the band. On New Year's Eve 1957 she passed out on the stage. "It took four people to hold me down for the shots necessary to calm my nerves that night," she said later. Anyone who understood the road learned to overlook comparatively minor flare-ups and concentrated on the big picture, the way an artist treated her musicians on the whole and the way the musicians treated the artist.

Jack Wilson recalls an engagement in which this mutual respect and help was shown at its best. "We were on the stage at Town Hall in Philadelphia, doing a show that included Lee Morgan and Phil Woods's Quintet, Sonny Rollins's Trio, and the Modern Jazz Quartet. Dinah used to finish with 'I'll Close My Eyes'—that was her finale. She'd take a note from the piano and tell me to give her an A, and I'd hit A on the piano and she'd start singing from there. Well, the concert had been going so good that all of a sudden she went right into the introduction to 'I'll Close My Eyes' without checking the note first. I reached down and hit the note and discovered that instead of the A she was supposed to be on, she had started with C, which means that the music that we had written in the key of C had to be transposed immediately up to E-flat, a minor third up. Now, it's one thing to transpose music up a half step, but to be able to transpose it up a minor third was difficult, and she was already into the song and couldn't change it. So, I found out what the key was while she was in the introduction and hollered very softly to the cats in the band, 'E-flat,' and those cats sight-read that music. The arrangement had a modulation in it; it went from C to D-flat. In this case, it went from E-flat to E, and they read the modulation. But, here's the kicker, it went down without a hitch. All the cats sight-read their music and the house came down. But as Dinah was taking her bow, she turned around and looked at the band, and the expression on her face was one of complete thankfulness. You can imagine what would have happened if Dinah Washington had messed up. And she turned around and looked at all of us, and it was very touching to see the expression on her face. It was like she let us see some vulnerability that we had not seen before, and I think that we all got a little closer to her at that point because she knew that we had saved her butt.

''Meanwhile, at the intermission, we found out that the promoter of the concert ran off with the money. Nobody could find him, and after the gig everybody went out and camped outside this cat's door, and baby, he ain't showed yet. But Dinah paid us. The rest of the people didn't get paid, but Dinah paid us. That's the way she was.''

The band at that time included Chamblee, Wilson, Davis,

Johnny Coles, Julian Priester, Westley Landers, and Richard Evans. They traveled in a sedan and a station wagon. "She loved Chrysler products. Lee Iaccoca would have loved Dinah," says Jack Wilson. The station wagon pulled a trailer containing the instruments and Dinah's extensive wardrobe. "She carried a lot of clothes, that's why she needed such a big trailer," says Charles Davis. "She put on fashion shows all over the place for us. She'd have a party and whatnot and she'd put on this, and this, and this. She said she always carried, and bought, a lot of clothes because when she was with Hampton she had to buy Gladys's old clothes." The musicians agreed that Dinah had excellent taste in clothes. Says Jack Wilson, "There are some singers now who can't dress worth a damn. They look like they're wearing creations from Omar the Tentman. Dinah was always wearing the latest fashions—she was wearing Gucci stuff before a lot of black people even knew who Gucci was, and a lot of white people, too. And she used to give a lot of dresses away to singers who were coming up—Gloria Lynne was the recipient of a lot of Dinah's gifts—and it wasn't stuff to be sneezed at, it was high-class stuff."

Although Dinah never ceased to rely on her favorite boosters in most of the towns where she played, and was always tickled when she could get a bargain, she also had legitimate dressmakers, among them Ethel White in New York, who was also Ernestine McClendon's dressmaker. "Ethel used to tell me that we were shaped just alike. We were both short-waisted, with no behind and no hips, and she used to have to do things to both of us to camouflage that," says McClendon. "Dinah and I would sometimes meet at Ethel's and she used to talk about men and how because she was free-hearted and good they tried to use her. She said she always tried to be a step ahead, but sometimes it would just get to her. But most of the time Ethel would be at Dinah's or at my place or backstage somewhere dressing one of us. Dinah and I used to be a little jealous of the time Ethel gave to the other. Ethel used to say that she made more trips to Dinah and me than to anybody else. She'd say, 'Both of you are lazy bitches, and I have to lug all this stuff around.' Ethel used to have to follow you around because she never finished anything, though it looked beautiful. She'd pin it on you and sew it, and when you'd get in the dressing room, she was still fixing and sewing. I remember Dinah saying once, 'Now look, bitch, I don't want no more motherfucking pins sticking in me when I go to dress. I've got a scar on the right side of my stomach from pins in the zipper. I pulled the zipper up and pulled all these pins up with it.'

"Ethel used to say about her, 'That evil bitch. I'd better have this ready before she comes. You can wait, but I've got to get hers ready.' And I remember one time Dinah came in, and Ethel was working on me, and Dinah looked at Ethel and said, 'No wonder I can't get my things. You're working on her all the time.' And yet there was the time when Ethel was working on a strapless gown for me and I didn't have a bra that would fit that gown. Ethel pulled out one of Dinah's, and I said she'd better call Dinah and ask her first, and Dinah said, 'She's my sister. Tell her if she wants it, she can have it, because I've got several of them.' That's the way she was.''

Of course, in Dinah's mind, there were Sisters, and then there were sisters. On occasion, one of the musicians would meet a girl on the road and want to bring her along, but one of Dinah's hard-and-fast rules was no women in the cars. "And," says Jack Wilson, "she would kind of pass judgment on our little girlfriends that we met along the way. You could tell whether she liked a woman or not, and the nicer the woman would try to be to Dinah, the more taciturn Dinah would be. I think Dinah had a lot of insecurity from the years when they called her Alligator because she had bad skin as a child. She felt insecure around pretty women. I remember one time we were working in Detroit, and there was a shake dancer in the show, a fine lady, and Dinah got her off the show. She was too fine, and Dinah canceled her out. Actually, it had a lot to do with personality. If a woman was fine and had an attitude, I think Dinah would pick up on it and zero in on it. A lady I was going with at the time was a very attractive woman, and Dinah liked her.'' Eddie Chamblee recalls a time when Dinah paid a girl's hospital expenses when she had a baby.

Slappy White agrees that there were some women Dinah did like. "Dinah was the cause of my marrying La Vern," he says, referring to La Vern Baker, who at the time was a major Rhythm and Blues star for Atlantic Records, with such hits as "I Cried a Tear" and "Jim Dandy." "I was on the road with Dinah when I met La Vern. Dinah had gone, and I stayed over in Washington, D.C. La Vern had seen me work somewhere and she was doing all the jokes I used to tell in her routine, and I stayed over to see her at this theater, and that's how we met. We struck it off, and I took her out to dinner, and then we went to Florida. Dinah said, 'Why don't you marry her?' I wasn't ready to get married, but I married her. But I still went on the road with Dinah. Then La Vern got hot and then I went on the road with La Vern. La Vern paid me the biggest salary I ever got. She gave me the first one thousand a week." Dinah never held it against Slappy or La Vern that their marriage caused her to lose the companionship of her longtime friend. Slappy had been with her for ten years, but nothing lasted forever.

Of course, Dinah was particularly vigilant with her own man—Eddie Chamblee at the time, but also any man whom she considered her escort. "She always felt that people picked at her," says LaRue Manns. "If she had a man with her, she'd declare that he was liking some other woman better than her, 'Cause I saw him looking at her.' Maybe he knew her and just wanted to speak to her, but not around Dinah: 'Hey, that's who you want? Well, you go over there and be with her. I thought you were with me.' She wanted that man to pay attention strictly to her and not look at anyone else or talk to anyone else unless she said he could. She'd say, 'You can talk to so-and-so. That's a friend of mine.' But they couldn't talk too long or she'd come back and say, 'What y'all talking about? Me?' She just had that deep inferiority complex.''

Jack Wilson recalls, ''I thought Dinah was a pretty woman after I got to know her, but she was not what you'd call a beauty. Contrary to popular belief, she was not a big woman. I think that was the image she projected, but she was only about five foot six or seven. All that weight she'd put on at one time in her life made her look even fatter because she was short.''

At that time, most, if not all, of the members of her band were younger than Dinah, who was in her early thirties. Also, she was married to Eddie Chamblee, so the subject of her attractiveness did not come up in their minds a lot, though it continued to come up in Dinah's. They were more interested in their careers, and being with Dinah helped to further their careers, not only by giving them experience and the opportunity to make superb recordings, but also, occasionally, allowing them to play in some venues that they might not otherwise have. Jack Wilson recalls, ''We were just coming off that recording session [in 1957, not long after he had joined Dinah's band; he believes it was around September 1957] when Dinah told us we were play-ing at Birdland, and that was a big thrill. Then, on the way to Birdland, we were told we were going to play Carnegie Hall the same night. Baby, that was something! We went into Birdland, and naturally all the cats in the band were thrilled to death, because we'd been hearing about Birdland all our lives. I still have a picture of me playing there in my scrapbook. Everything went beautifully, and they broadcast it over "Monitor," which I think was on NBC; they'd go around to nightclubs on the weekends and you might hear Count Basie or anybody. It was on late at night, two or three A.M.—live music coming from some club."

Dinah came to love Birdland. Whenever she was in New York, if she wasn't performing at Birdland, she was in the audience. She and Morris Levy, owner of Birdland, were close, but Leonard Feather tells the story that Dinah and the emcee at the club were not. "There was this little guy named Pee Wee Marquette, who was a midget and who would announce all the artists there. He was sort of the emcee, and he took a little money on the side from everybody, too, saying he'd take care of them, which meant he'd given them a decent announcement and treat them well. Dinah didn't like that kind of thing; she didn't want to have to be bribing this guy. So Pee Wee gives this long buildup about, 'We now give you one of the great singers of all time and here she is ladies and gentlemen, Ruth Jones.' I don't know if that's true or not, but it's a good story. I saw her at Birdland many times; she was very popular there."

Wilson continues, "And the same day, that next night, we were at Carnegie Hall. We didn't have time to get nervous; it was like being on the road, get off the stand, pack up, and go on to the next gig."

From Birdland, "Monitor," and Carnegie Hall to Pittsburgh. That was not their itinerary, but it could have been. As entertainers, who spent most of their time on the road, they never knew where they would be from one week to the next. And as black entertainers they never knew when they would come up against prejudice. Sometimes it happened in the most unexpected places. "One time we were in Pittsburgh unloading in front of the club," says Jack

Wilson. "A cop comes by, a white cop, and he's drunk. Literally, the cop was drunk. He told us to get out of there, and we told him we were unloading our instruments, and one thing led to another and he arrested everybody in the band. Dinah came down and bailed us out and cursed out the whole police force.

"Another time, we were in Laurel, Mississippi, had driven all the way from Houston, Texas, to Mississippi. It's summertime and we're hot and sticky and we go to the one black motel, and it's full except for one room, and we give that to Dinah. We can't stay in the white hotels, so we decide to go to the gig, unload the instruments, and try to find a place to wash up. The gig is in an old corrugated steel barn, and the piano strings are sticking out of the piano, and the bass player gets up on stage, and while he's tuning up the bass, two strings break. And we have to put on white shirts and clean suits over all this grime because we can't find a place to take a shower.

"In those cases, there wasn't anything Dinah could do. She'd just have to finesse it. But there was a time in Miami Beach, I'll never forget. There was a white man in the audience who insulted her racially. We were in this big room—it was called the Livingroom, I think—and she grabbed a chair and put this chair in front of the man and sat down in this chair in front of him and started singing a slow blues. And the guys in the band, we knew it was kind of extraordinary, and when we looked over at her, we saw that her eyes were filled with tears. And she's singing the blues to this cat. I don't even know if it reached him, he was such a zurch. But she knew that was the only thing she could do. She'd gotten a bad rap a lot of times, because of what she did, but in more times than one Dinah knew what was happening and judged the situation right."

The possibility that something might be done about segregation in America was becoming real by then. In Mont-

gomery, Alabama, in the late 1950s, blacks had stayed off
the city buses in protest and won the right to sit wherever
they wanted to. A young Baptist minister named Martin
Luther King, Jr., had emerged from that boycott a major
civil rights leader, and Dinah became very close to him,
calling him often and sending money to help him in his
various causes. "She kept up with what was going on,"
says LaRue Manns. "She thought it was beautiful and she
used to say, 'I may not see it, but someday things will be
better.' She always had it in her heart that things would
open up and we could walk into hotels and have a nice suite
and go sit in the dining room and all of that." Dinah had
not been known in her life for fighting discrimination, but
she had done what she could. Other successful black entertainers, among them Nat King Cole, were charged with
being Uncle Toms and not doing enough for the struggle,
but there was never any question that Dinah was proud of
being black and willing to help in the cause. Says Ernestine
McClendon, "It was just the way she would say, 'My sister
. . . my brother.' And she used to do a lot of free benefits
for black people. My husband said he used to get a show
together and a lot of these bitches don't want to do nothing,
but the white folks ask them, they jump over the moon,
you know? But Dinah was always ready to do a free benefit."

Still, Dinah was not a crusader for causes. She had
enough trouble keeping her own life and career together.
And even if she'd decided to devote the time to the burgeoning civil rights movement, it is unlikely that she would
have lasted long, given the nonviolent philosophy of the
movement. Dinah was not a turn-the-other-cheek type of
person, her actions in Miami Beach that time notwithstanding. She was a fighter, and because she could have little
effect on the big issues, she turned her fighting skills on
those closest to her, on those who loved her most. Like

Eddie Chamblee. People who were around them during the time they were married recall that they argued a lot. ''I vaguely remember him,'' says Patti Austin, ''and I vaguely remember a lot of arguing going on between them. I never really was in on any of them because Dinah always protected me from that kind of unpleasantness. She'd give me that Black Mama look, which meant, 'Get the hell outa this room.' She'd just kind of tap me on the shoulder and nod, meaning, 'You, out!' I didn't feel badly, I knew it was just her way. I figured it was something I wasn't supposed to know about. I was never a child who asked, 'Why?' Having a black mother, you never ask why—'why' will get you killed. But I do remember her and one of her husbands— it could have been Eddie Chamblee—getting ready to have a *serious* argument, and she sent me out of the room with 'Patti, why don't you go play with the kids.' I went in the other room with the boys, and I remember us all leaning at the door so we could hear what was going on. We stayed there maybe fifteen or twenty seconds, and we heard arguing. And we all looked at each other and rolled our eyes and kind of went back and played. Those crazy adults, you know. That was really the wildest it ever got when I was there. Not knowing the basis for an argument, it was out of context for me, so it wasn't that interesting. It certainly wasn't anything I wanted to get in the middle of.''

LaRue Manns recalls, ''Oh, yes, they would have falling outs. That was because Eddie was one of the husbands who really was a man in his own right. He didn't marry her for her bright lights and good living. He already had that. He was a star in his own world. But she felt that he should be more dependent on her. With the band, he was the leader of the band, but she wanted to be the engineer, and they would have professional conflicts. She would have pros and cons about the band, and he would tell her that it was his band and he knew what was best and how to do the music.

But he gave her every break that was possible."

Two years later and in a bitter mood, Dinah gave a different story to Dave Hepburn for his article. "He soon began to show me he resented me. He thought I was bossing the band and went into tantrums to show me who was boss. He berated me constantly and embarrassed me more than I care to remember. . . . I don't want to go into all the sordid details of our life together, but I have never felt so completely on the edge of a precipice as I did during that marriage."

The end for Dinah and Eddie came sometime in late 1958, in a club in Miami, Florida. Everybody was tired, having driven from New York to Florida. "I'd been driving and I was just exhausted," says Chamblee. "I was driving right behind him," says Charles Davis. Onstage, something happened, no one really remembers, though Dinah remembered that she was singing "Drowning in My Tears." "I guess I hit a lot of wrong notes," says Chamblee. The next thing anyone knew, according to Jack Wilson, "She picked up Eddie's brand-new Sylmar Mark IV tenor saxophone and threw it against a concrete wall, and it exploded into a bunch of pieces and looked like a *piñata* when it hit that wall."

Eddie Chamblee remembers, "I just walked off. If I'd waited two more minutes, it never would have happened [the breakup]. Because it was so silly. Just that one night when I was so tired. But even after I'd cooled down, I didn't go back—too proud."

Since Dinah and Eddie were in the habit of having knock-down-drag-out arguments one night and then acting like cooing newlyweds the next morning, the guys in the band fully expected to see Eddie return. "We got another saxophone player to play his part and continued to perform," says Charles Davis, "After a certain period of time, we realized Eddie wasn't coming back. It was the first time *that* had happened onstage. It had nothing to do with notes, it was something else, because he was a marvelous saxophonist. Whatever they were going through wasn't about notes.''

In Eddie Chamblee's opinion, it was about control, and it went all the way back to Dinah's problems with her mother. ''All her life Dinah wanted her mother to love her. And in a man Dinah was looking for love, for total, complete acceptance that she never got from her mother. The mother was dominating. Dinah resisted. The conflict was, Who's going to rule the roost? Dinah was not a complicated woman if you knew the bottom line.''

Eddie Chamblee returned to New York and moved his belongings out of Dinah's apartment at the Bowery Bank Building and back into the small apartment that he had always kept, even while they were married—''that was one of my little shenanigans.'' To this day, a small part of him regrets that he left in anger—''if I'd just waited two more minutes . . .'' Later, they almost got back together. ''It was in the islands, I don't remember which ones. I was playing down there, and Dinah was down there on vacation. This was a few months later. We talked about getting married again, but it was the same confusion; we had different ideas about things and knew that wasn't going to change.''

Dinah always regretted the breakup, too, although sometimes when she got on the subject of how men had used her throughout her life, she was inclined to lump Eddie Chamblee in with the rest of them. She told Charles Sanders of *Ebony* not long before she died, ''[That marriage] is the one that I thought would really last. He told me he wouldn't marry me until I asked him. I waited and then we both laughed. I thought he was joking, but he wasn't . . . so, you guessed it, I asked! But after a while, Eddie and I agreed to disagree, and that was that.''

''I remember going to her apartment one time and expecting to see Eddie Chamblee,'' says Gordon Austin, ''but there was someone else there. I thought, 'She's done it again.' I kept on doing what I was doing, talking to her and laughing. She wined and dined me—cooked a beautiful dinner. But after a while I said I was tired and was going back to my hotel and to bed.'' Even people who knew Dinah well were often taken aback by the frequent changes in her romantic relationships.

There were a lot of strangers for a while. Dinah never lacked for a man, but many were rent-a-husbands, for the moment. Patti Austin calls them ''window dressing.'' ''The short relationships she'd have would be terribly romantic and lovable, I remember that. And Dinah was the eternal optimist—this was always going to be the one. But I think that was partly for my benefit. I think she was a serious closet crier. Now that I'm grown up, I realize that there were a lot of things she was going through that she would have done a lot of crying about.''

Blues of the Queen

As 1959 began, Dinah was feeling stuck in a rut, both personally and professionally. She would turn thirty-five that year and she worried about ever finding a man to grow old with. Although according to Gordon Austin, "Dinah always had a crowd of men around her." Professionally, she was saddled with the blues label. As Arnold Shaw, who was then creative head of E. B. Marks Music, wrote in the liner notes of *A Slick Chick on the Mellow Side*, "She possessed a greater scope than virtually all of her R&B compatriots, displaying an amazing ability to embrace many different types of song. In truth, her versatility proved a besetting limitation. Because of it, Mercury Records used her to reach black record-buyers with songs they normally might not buy. As soon as a disk showed promise of becoming a hit—country song, film theme, show tune, Tin-Pan Alley ballad—Dinah was rushed into the studio to make a cover for the black listeners. Although Dinah possessed the vocal artistry to have crossed over like a Roberta Flack or Diana Ross, Mercury kept her locked in an R&B cage, an area in which her pre-eminence is indicated by the dozens of disks that made R&B charts, most of them reaching the Top 5 to Top 1 slots."

Her friends and supporters in the music business were

eager to help her break out of the R&B mold. Leonard
Feather was one. He had followed her career closely since
that long-ago time when he and she had been "lucky to
each other," as he put it. Now a writer for *Billboard*, he
stated in early 1959 that Dinah "remains today a great blues
singer, but she is many other things, too—a unique inter-
preter of pop songs. . . ." To underscore the versatility of
Dinah's musical knowledge in the pop field, he asked her
to take a "blindfold test," playing a number of records
without telling her the names of the artists and asking for
her critical comments. While this was not the first time that
Dinah had submitted to one of Feather's blindfold tests, a
regular feature of his *Billboard* column, it is significant that
the nine songs he played for her were pop songs. But if the
column was aimed at helping the new Dinah reach a wider
public, it lost nothing of the old Dinah's keen ear and uninhibited comments:

*Eugenie Baird. "I Let a Song Go Out of My Heart."
(Design). Stereo. Arranged by Mercer Ellington; Ben Webster, tenor sax.* "I don't know who that was at all. She
really fixed Duke's song there—she fixed it but good. When
she came to that line 'to make amends,' I was thinking, the
only amends that can be made is to break the record! It
sounded in spots like Teddi King, but Teddi swings. . . .
I hope that isn't Teddi. You'll get no comment on the
accomplishment. I won't give that *any* stars."

*Ella Fitzgerald. "What's Your Story Morning Glory"
(Verve). Arranged and conducted by Marty Paich.* "That
was the First Lady, and I must say she sounded like her old
self—that pure soul. The arrangement was very nice. I heard
her do a few things a while back that didn't sound like the
Ella I know, but this certainly does. I'll give this five. I've
known Ella ever since she gave me a dress, when I started
out with Lionel Hampton. . . . Bless her heart—I sure needed
it, too. Incidentally, I didn't give her the five stars just
because she gave me the dress!"

Chet Baker. "Old Devil Moon" (Riverside). "Who the heck is that? Is that a singer or someone just kidding? I don't know who it is, but the diction is terrible. At the end it sounded like he said, 'That old bubble moon,' and I thought the words were 'old devil moon.' It sounds like he had a mouthful of mush. . . . I can't rate this. I thought it was the Velvet Fog for a minute, but I can't imagine who it was, unless it was Chet Baker."

Dinah's and Feather's mutual friend, Arnold Shaw, was also eager to help Dinah. When Clyde Otis became A&R (artist and repertory) man at Mercury, the first black to hold that position at a major record company, Shaw saw an opportunity. He brought a song called "What a Diff'rence a Day Made" to Otis and persuaded him to record it with Dinah. At the recording session with the Belford Hicks Orchestra, Dinah changed the tense of the verb and produced "What a Diff'rence a Day Makes."

Shaw was pleased with the recording, as were the Mercury executives. "But," recalls Shaw, "when it came to promoting the disk, Mercury sales executives limited their efforts to R&B disk jockeys and black sales outlets, as they had done with her other recordings. I was so convinced that Dinah's disk was a Pop hit that I personally went on a barnstorming tour although my firm, Edward B. Marks Music Corporation, employed regional promoters. In the course of my cross-country promo trip, I occasionally phoned Mercury execs both to tell them of the enthusiastic reaction of white dee jays as well as hopefully to motivate the company to widen its promotion efforts. It was of no avail. I was told that I was a misguided music man, that Dinah had a waiting audience in the country's black ghettoes [sic] for anything she recorded, and that her disks were good for a sale of 25,000 or more without Mercury making a single promotion call.

"Needless to say, the company execs were misled by their own preconceptions. Dinah's disk of 'What a Diff'-

rence a Day Makes' did cross over into the mainstream [it entered the pop charts on June 14, 1959], climbed to #9 on *Billboard's* pop Honor Roll of Hits, and finished in the 'Top 50 Hot Disks of the Year' at the same time that Dinah won a Grammy for the Best R&B Record of 1959. From then [on], while maintaining her black following, she was recognized as a top mainstream artist.''

It was just possible that after more than fifteen years in the business, Dinah had a chance to become a mainstream star. She was ready to exploit all possibilities. She changed her look and now featured a sleek hairstyle, with a straight ponytail, lots of glitter—rhinestone-studded hair clip, dangling earrings, cuff bracelet—satin gowns, white mink. She exuded glamour. She may have grown tired of being identified always as a blues singer, but she had never minded the Queen part.

She was not, however, getting the bookings that a mainstream artist ought to enjoy. ''She had a few hit records out, and one that was really hot, 'What a Diff'rence a Day Makes,' '' says Ruth Bowen, who became her agent, ''but she didn't have any work. Here she was with a top agency, and I went down and I spoke to Joe Glaser about it. I said, 'What is this? You can't get any work for this girl? She's hot as hell.' He had a meeting with his agents to fire them up, and I said, 'Well, if you people can't do it, I'll just have to do it myself.' ''

Although Dinah remained with Joe Glaser's Associated Booking Corp., she took on Ruth Bowen as a sort of personal manager. It was Bowen's first foray into the business, although she had been around the business since marrying Billy Bowen of the Ink Spots in 1944. She'd been friends with Dinah ever since they had first met in 1945 or 1946, and over the past several years Dinah had begun to urge her to utilize her many show business contacts in a business for herself. At length, Bowen had begun to listen to Dinah and had been studying Joe Glaser's operation with that idea in the back of her mind.

"I learned a great deal from Joe Glaser because he was king of the agents—he was like the daddy of the agencies. He had a habit of sitting down in his office by himself on a Saturday to sign his mail—he always signed every letter that was sent out, and he licked his own stamps. I'd go down and I'd sit with him on Saturdays to just sort of talk to him. Then one day he decided, 'You're picking my brain. That's why you come down here. You don't come to visit me.' So he gave me a lot of good pointers, and he admired me for my spunk and everything. We became good friends. He never represented my husband; I got close to him through Dinah.

"Dinah's not getting work wasn't his fault—Joe Glaser could pick up the phone and do anything. It was his agents. If nobody called, they didn't push it, they didn't try to sell her too hard. I can't say that it was because she was black. A lot of them didn't really like Dinah—her ways, you know? She'd call and cuss 'em out. A couple of them adored her—Joe Sully, who's still around in the business, and Oscar Cohen tried to do their best. But they didn't understand the business that well. They were accustomed to the Benny Goodmans and the big names that they could book with ease."

So, Ruth Bowen began to see what she could do for Dinah. "We never had a contract, no signed agreement. We never had one argument. I told her in the beginning, because I understood that she wasn't the easiest person to get along with, 'If you respect me enough to ask me to do this, then you must respect me when I give you advice. If we have to argue, we don't need each other.' She always remembered that. We'd get angry at each other, but we never argued. We just didn't speak."

Dinah felt that, as a mainstream artist, she ought to go

to Europe, but the agents at Associated Booking Corp. couldn't seem to line up anything for her, or didn't try. "I made a few calls," says Bowen. "I was very fortunate because in traveling with my husband I'd made a lot of friends throughout the world. I picked up the phone and called a promoter in Sweden, and he booked a few European dates for her. And she called Joe Glaser and said, 'You see? Don't tell me what can't be done.'"

Bowen did not accompany Dinah on that first trip to Europe. LaRue went, as did pianist Beryl Booker and assorted valets, maids, and hairdressers. The seven-piece band had broken up after Dinah and Eddie Chamblee had parted and Jack Wilson was drafted. "She decided to go back to a trio," says Charles Davis, who went to California for a while, then returned to New York and played with Kenny Doyle. "She'd call me every once in a while to do a gig." Bowen was pleased not to have to make arrangements for a large entourage in England, but she was still concerned about how Dinah would comport herself there. "I was giving her instructions about what not to do in England," Bowen recalls, "and I said, 'Dinah, whatever you do, don't make any remarks about the queen. Now, they don't take kindly to that over there.' The first day out, LaRue called and said, 'Well, she did it.' And I said, 'What?' LaRue said, 'She walked out on the stage and got a standing ovation, and when the audience quieted down, she said, "Ladies and gentlemen, I'm happy to be here, but just remember, there's one heaven, one earth, and one queen, and your Elizabeth is an imposter." I wanted to die, but they loved it.' She had them in the palm of her hand, the way she did it."

Also in London, Dinah was again "lucky" for Leonard Feather. "I was there on a visit, and the BBC was putting on a special program of all my compositions and I was supposed to have Helen Merrill singing a couple of numbers on the show. But at rehearsal, Helen Merrill didn't show up at the studio. I ran into Dinah on the street, with Beryl Booker, the great black piano player, and I said, 'My goodness, maybe you can help me out. I'm supposed to do this radio show, and Helen Merrill didn't show up. Do you think you can help out and do it?' Very kindly, Dinah immediately agreed to step in, and she never asked about the money or anything. So, she came into the studio and sang 'Evil Gal Blues' on this radio show—no preparation or anything.''

From London, Dinah went on to Stockholm, where—although she had been away from home for only about a month—she decided she was lonely for her latest flame, Horatio "Rusty" Maillard, whom she'd left back in New York. The press always identified him as a New York cabdriver, which not a few of Dinah's fans refused to believe. But according to LaRue Manns, "He really was a New York cabdriver. He was bringing us home one night, and she met him and she sort of fell for him. She was lonely.''

Back in New York, Ruth Bowen got a call from Dinah. "She said, 'What is my marital status?' She wanted to marry Rusty. I sent him over to Europe C.O.D. First time that the airline had ever permitted it. She said, 'I'll pay when he arrives.' ''

LaRue Manns recalls, "She was supposedly madly in love with the guy, and they wanted to get married. We were in Stockholm, Sweden, and they hadn't spent enough time in the country to be able to get married. But she wanted to get married anyway—at sea. So she just bought the rings and announced that they'd gotten married." According to the press releases, Dinah Washington and Rusty Maillard were married in international waters off Stockholm. LaRue was matron of honor and Stefan Landerol, a Swedish saxophone player, was best man. "When we got back to the United States, the record company gave them a fabulous wedding reception," says Manns. Actually, it was Morris

Levy, former owner of Birdland, who had just started a new record company, Roulette, who gave the lavish party at the Round Table Club. A great fan of Dinah's, he was trying to lure her away from Mercury, but she remained loyal to Mercury.

Talking to Dave Hepburn about Maillard, Dinah did not try to pretend that he was something other than what he was. "Rusty has been a cabdriver," she said, "and if he wanted to continue in this job, I would be glad to let him, but I need business help and I want him near me. I pay him a salary, and he handles my affairs with intelligence and thoroughness." Dinah described Rusty as "a fine, upstanding young man" who showed "a great love for my kids. He took them out, saw that they attended school, and did a lot of little things for me. He is kind, thoughtful and gentle. I hope this is for keeps."

On Dinah's return to the United States, Mercury had a heavy recording schedule lined up for her. Some critics felt that Mercury overreacted to Dinah's success by pushing her into recordings that were too mainstream. A case in point was a session in Los Angeles in 1961 in which Dinah, accompanied by piano, guitar, bass, drum, and strings, recorded ten sides, mostly motion picture themes arranged and conducted by Belford Hicks. These recordings were not released until 1967, several years after Dinah's death, on an album called *Dinah Discovered.* Stanley Dance, reviewing the album for *Stereo Review,* wrote, "Miss Washington's popularity grew inexplicably as her accompaniments worsened. Here she is burdened with a ludicrous string ensemble. . . . Perhaps the contrast itself, as between her sere voice and the sickly backgrounds, was what appeared to the masses, but her best work, like Billie Holiday's, was done with small uncompromising jazz groups. A potentially fine rhythm section is given little scope. . . ."

The only successful new venue that Mercury engineered

for Dinah was her duets with Brook Benton, the first of
which she recorded around the same time as "What a Diff'-
rence a Day Makes." Benton, who was in his late twenties
at the time, had recently signed with Mercury Records,
thanks no doubt to Clyde Otis, Mercury's A&R man. He
had gotten his start with Bill Landford's Spiritual Quartet
and in recent years had collaborated with Clyde Otis, who
had started out as a songwriter, to produce several hit songs,
including "Looking Back" for Nat King Cole and "Lover's
Question" for Clyde McPhatter. His voice blended nicely
with Dinah's, and there was a man-woman electricity between them that came through with great sensuality in the
duets. Arnold Shaw, who attended some of those studio
sessions, described the Dinah of the duets as a "tantalizing
kitten." So far as is known, however, Dinah and Brook
Benton never got more intimate than singing to each other
in the studio. Dinah was quite content with Rusty Maillard
at the time.

It may have been to "keep" Rusty Maillard that Dinah
got serious about losing weight. Or perhaps it was a professional decision. Whatever the reason, Patti Austin believes
that it was not a decision that the Dinah she'd known well
would have made. "I don't think she felt she was an ugly
duckling. If anything, I felt she felt she was the finest bitch
on the planet. I guess if I look back, in retrospect that might
have been a terrible inferiority complex that she was cov-
ering up by being cocky. But in my recollection, Dinah was
very fond of herself. I don't remember her ever looking
in a mirror and looking disappointed. I do remember her
looking in the mirror and primping her ass off and saying,
'Ooo, girl, too cute.' Now, she might have done that just
for me. . . . But I don't think so. You have to remember
that when I met her, she was really at the peak of her career,
and being svelte wasn't really the big focus at that time. If
you look at the women who were really popular then, by

today's standards they're hogs. She didn't give a shit about being heavy—just make me a bigger dress, you know. But by around 1960, it was starting to be important to be svelte, and she said, that's it, I gotta lose weight, gotta get thin, keep up with the times.''

With the success of ''What a Diff'rence a Day Makes'' and her duets with Brook Benton, Dinah had the best shot she'd had since her career began to make it in mainstream American music, not to mention other mainstream areas, such as advertising. Dinah actually got to appear in a Rheingold beer ad in 1959: ''No one can copy my blues—or my beer!'' To be sure, the ad only appeared in black publications, among them *Ebony* in October 1959. Dinah, Queen of the Blues, had to share space with an inset touting *The Jackie Robinson Show* on WRCA-Radio, sponsored by Rheingold. But there was no question in Dinah's mind that the possibilities for such commercial endorsements would be further heightened by a more mainstream image.

Whatever her reasons, Dinah Washington shed close to fifty pounds in the course of a few months in 1959–60. She told *Ebony* that the weight loss was the result of a new diet that permitted her ''to eat everything I want, including pig's feet and all that kind of food that isn't found in most restaurants'' and reducing pills taken after meals, which she tried to confine to two a day. They were heavy meals, she said—Italian food ''until I feel it running out of my ears'' and her beloved soul food. She told *Ebony* that she had dropped from 174 to 128 and taken four inches off her bust, six inches off her waist, and five inches off her hips.

Reducing pills were not her only weapon against weight. She neglected to mention that she was also taking mercury injections. According to LaRue Manns, these were given her by the same doctor who had first started prescribing pills for her weight loss, Dr. Harry K. Stone. Says Manns, ''He showed her how to give them to herself, because I refused.'' The injections drew water out of her system and had astonishing effects. ''Like, maybe today she's a ten and she has a size-eight dress that she wants to wear tonight. One shot, and she had to stay near the bathroom for several hours, but by the time she was ready to go out, nine or ten o'clock at night, she could wear that size-eight dress.

''She'd be all hyped up, and then she'd drink on top of that. Then when she came in at three or four o'clock in the morning, she'd be high and she'd go for her sleeping pills, to go to sleep. But she'd be all hyped up from the alcohol and whatever else was in her system and she'd sleep for an hour and then she'd wake up and start walking. Then she'd go take another sleeping pill, and sometimes maybe she'd take two instead of one, and she might sleep for two-three hours. When she'd wake up, she'd be all disagreeable— 'What's all that noise out there?' I'd say, 'What noise? Nobody out here but me. I can't stop the noise in the street.' ''

It is ironic that Dinah should turn to these drugs so soon after the death of Billie Holiday, whose life and career were ruined by heroin. Billie had long been her idol, and over the years they had become good friends. The story goes that Dinah once missed a gig in Brooklyn and sent Billie in her place. ''That might have been true,'' says LaRue Manns. ''They were very good friends. Billie was never up to this place [the Bowery Building], but they were telephone visitors, talked all the time. And whenever we were in a town and she was there, we would stop and see her. Sometimes she remembered, sometimes she'd forget, you know. You know Billie. They tried all they could to talk her out of it, but she'd say, 'Girl, I can't do without it.' '' Dinah was deeply saddened by Billie's death, but it did not surprise her. She always made a distinction between the street drugs that killed Billie and the prescription drugs she took. And hers were always prescription, thanks to her accommodating doctor.

Unfortunately, Rusty Maillard wasn't around very long to appreciate the new, svelte Dinah. Less than a year after their "marriage," Dinah put him out. LaRue Manns recalls, "She got angry with him and put him out, and then he called the press and told them the real story. Then she calls me from California and wakes me up at four o'clock in the morning to say, 'Maisie—(she used to call me Maisie) if you get any calls, tell them the truth. We weren't married.'"

Eventually they made up, Ruth Bowen recalls. "She was friends with all her husbands and 'husbands.' They all loved her, regardless. Even Walter Buchanan, who sued her for alimony. They talked. She'd call him a few names, but she talked to him. Jimmy Cobb and Eddie Chamblee were my favorites. They loved her. I remember one night. When she'd come home from a trip, she always loved to go out on the town, especially to Birdland, and I was coming from a dinner or somewhere, coming across One hundred and twenty-fifth Street heading to the West Side Drive, and I stopped for a light and I saw Dinah in her car with five of her husbands. They were all out partying! They worked together a lot."

By this time, Ruth Bowen and Dinah had gone into partnership and opened their own agency. Appropriately, it was called Queen Artists Corp. "After I got her the bookings in Europe, she started encouraging me to start an office," Bowen recalls. "She said, 'Why should you do the work and somebody else make the money?' So I started the agency with very little money." Dinah was the first client, but they had no trouble attracting others, though they were not big-time stars. "The big agencies wanted big acts, so a lot of the up-and-coming acts kind of got lost in the shuffle. And that was one of the reasons for our success, because we'd take the unknowns and make them. We started with very little money, and it was hard to battle the big agencies, so I started to come in another way. So I booked a lot of jazz acts, organ trios—I had every organ trio that you can imagine—the Kenny Burrells. Dinah discovered the Dells.''

LaRue Manns shared the operation of the booking agency with Bowen. By this time, Manns had moved to an apartment of her own in the Bowery Building: ''That was in 1959,'' says Manns. ''My mother at that time was sick, and I went to Pittsburgh to bring her here to have the doctors check her out. She stayed with me in my bedroom because over there we had three bedrooms. The doctor told her she needed to be where she would have plenty of rest, and that was not at Dinah's, with the kids playing drums and the records going and Dinah hollering and singing and the pots and pans banging in the kitchen. Mother enjoyed it, but it wasn't getting her well. So I said, 'Dinah, I have to get an apartment. Either that or I'm gonna take off and go back home with mother.' She said, 'No, you're not going,' and Dinah put on her mink coat and her gown and went downstairs to the office and said, 'I need another apartment and I want it on the same side.' But they didn't have any that were empty; this was the only one. We came over here, and she said, 'I'll take it,' and we got a few things in here—a bed and a phone. And then I began to fix it up, and I've been here ever since.''

Even after her mother went back to Pittsburgh, LaRue kept the apartment. ''As the boys got older, like twelve or thirteen, they wanted their own room. So I [kept this] so they could have their own room and be with her. When she was out of town, I would use her bedroom.'' Manns continued to oversee Dinah's contracts, do her banking, and pay the bills. Poor health prevented her from traveling very often with Dinah, so it was logical that she should be involved in the agency. ''Joe Glaser was still her agent,'' says Manns. ''We were like her managers, Ruth was her personal manager and kept the contracts and dealt with Glaser. All Dinah had to do was go to work, get off the plane, and go where she was going and work. I helped with the other office work and managed the different artists. We had a girl singer, Dolores Coleman—beautiful girl—but she got hung up on dope. I understand that she died. We had some name jazz groups, and then from that we went into rhythm and blues and rock and roll. We had the Allegros, who went on to make records and did very well. We had quite a few, and we would try to book them behind Dinah or through another agency for a percentage.''

No doubt, the new agency helped to keep Dinah's mind off her love problems, though by the time she put Rusty Maillard out, she already had another lover. She *always* had another lover, if for no other reason than to keep from being bored. She also had a large entourage of people, whom she kept around primarily to amuse her. Robert Richards was working as an illustrator in Boston when Dinah played the club Storeyville in that city. He was in his late teens, with a ready wit, and Dinah liked him and invited him to go on the road with her. ''I was saved from banality by Dinah,'' Richards told Leslie Gourse, author of *Louis' Children*. ''Basically she supported me because I left my job to go with her. We were just friends. Later I lived with her in Harlem. It was the most incredible experience for me. Dinah was unique. She had one lover right after another. And her house was like a depot. There was always something going on, people dealing and trading in God knows what all.''

Dinah's world had long been like that; the difference was that now the men with whom she surrounded herself were usually much younger than she. Her next husband, Rafael Campos, was Ferris Kimbrough's age, or about thirteen years younger than Dinah. Apparently, they met while Dinah was in Los Angeles performing and recording early in 1961. It was a whirlwind courtship, and they were married shortly thereafter. ''She was married to him in Mexico,'' says LaRue Manns, ''and at that time I don't think that was considered really legal, until they got remarried in the United States. But anyway, they got married." Campos, a handsome young man, appeared in movies and on TV. Dinah decided to introduce him to musical stage audiences, which the critic for *Variety* did not find amusing. "House Review: Apollo, N.Y.," May 17, 1961: "Apollo's management should be chided for billing Rafael Campos as a special guest star during the vaudery's current frame. Campos, himself a talented actor and husband of topliner Dinah Washington, is made to stand around and nibble at his frau's ear during one of her several otherwise successful numbers. If that's what the Apollo calls a 'duet,' then the theatre works from an unfamiliar showbiz lexicon." The Eddie Chamblee Orchestra backed Dinah on this gig, with no fewer than seven violins. Chamblee was also acting as her road manager at this time. One thing that can be said for Dinah—she may have lost a few men as husbands, but she never lost them as friends and fellow professionals.

Ruth Bowen had a unique way of keeping track of Dinah's husbands—"I kept a file on husbands." To place the Rafael Campos period exactly, she would have to go to her file, but she does remember that Campos was at Dinahland. This was the former Robert's Show Club (also known as Robert's Show Lounge) on the South Side of Chicago, a jazz club that had been in business for some years and at which she had played often when she was in Chicago. For a brief time she took over operation of the club and changed its name to Dinahland. According to the press, during the first month, she featured herself as the main attraction and did well. But after that she had to go on the road, and the acts she booked were less-than-name acts. Attendance began to drop off, and after ten weeks Herman Roberts, the original owner, took the club back, charging that Dinah had relinquished it "by default." Roberts booked Brook Benton and Nina Simone in for the next two weeks and succeeded in getting his customers back. Ruth Bowen tells another story. "Dinah had a habit of inviting everybody, every performer, over to catch the show, and of course she'd always pick up the tab and just have a big party, close the doors, and everybody would get up and perform and have a ball. And I would have to fly in every weekend with some funds to pay off the help because Dinah hadn't taken in any money. Campos was at Dinahland."

No one could figure that marriage out, except Patti Austin, who was entering adolescence and beginning to appreciate men. "I thought he was the finest sucker I'd ever seen in my life, and I remember telling her, 'Ooo, he's cute,' because I was at the age when little girls say that. I thought he was just gorgeous, the hottest thing since cookies. As I look back on it, I think I was influenced by her. I remember the way she introduced him, '*This is my* new husband. Isn't he fine?' And I'd say, 'Yeah, he's fine, he's fine.' I think half the reason I thought he was fine is that she kept telling me he was. She was into the *fineness* of this man; she wore him like a necklace. He always treated me like a princess, so I adored him, and I was so sad when that didn't work. And that was the only husband that I recall that I really cared about, that I really liked."

Patti's father, Gordon Austin, liked him, too, but didn't take the marriage seriously. "I felt sorry for him because he was so little." According to LaRue Manns, even Dinah used to laugh about the marriage. "She had fun with that marriage, and it was beautiful while it lasted. But he was so much younger than she was, and she began to feel self-conscious. [Dinah's] boys would say, 'He ain't much bigger than I am—I can wear his clothes.' In the end, she began to get jealous of him because he was so friendly. And he couldn't endure the life she wanted—one-night stands and her seeing ten other men, because she liked to play around. He didn't like it. So he just got into his car one day and rolled away.'' The marriage lasted only a matter of months. Said Dinah of her sixth husband, ''All I have to say about him is that he couldn't even pretend that he loved me.'' Manns recalls, ''They continued to be friends after that. He came to see her. It was beautiful while it lasted.''

''I change husbands before they change me,'' Dinah once told Leonard Feather, but the flippancy of that remark masked a deep personal despair that she would never find a man who loved her for herself, and who loved her enough not to let her walk all over him. She seemed especially discouraged in 1961, and whether it was because she felt foolish for having married Rafael Campos at all or because she was tired from nearly twenty years on the road, no one who knew her well can guess. They know only that things seemed to be coming apart for Dinah Washington.

In addition to taking mercury injections and pills of all sorts for all kinds of reasons, she was drinking heavily. In June, she was hospitalized briefly in Philadelphia for treatment of anemia, but she could not afford to take a much-needed rest.

Dinah's health, and her responsibilities, weighed on her mind, and her emotional fuse was shorter than usual over the next few months as she maintained her heavy road schedule and worried over unpaid bills and wondered when she was ever going to be able to slow down. Although Dinah put on an attitude of typical bravado, for the musicians who traveled with her, life could be a nightmare, and during this time she went through accompanists in the snap of a finger. Now that Dinah was recording almost exclusively with large orchestras, her instrumentalists had less opportunity for featured spots on her records, and without that advantage to outweigh the disadvantages of traveling with the mean Queen, there was little incentive for them to stay with her long.

Seattle-born pianist Patti Brown joined her on the spur of the moment in Los Angeles in late 1960. ''She was always the actress,'' Brown later told Leslie Gourse. ''She called me to go to work for her. She said, 'Bitch?' and I knew her voice. I hung up. She called back and said, 'This is Dinah Washington, Queen of the Blues.' She always called herself that. Rehearsal took place in a car on the way to Asbury Park. She told me the keys and the song she wanted to sing. That was the whole rehearsal.

''Then, during the show, she jumped around from key to key, and I followed her. I have perfect pitch. Then, on stage, she asked me to play a tune. But because the trio was at one end of a big, wide stage and she was at the other end, I couldn't hear her. So I said, 'Excuse me, Miss Washington,' and she said, 'Play so-and-so, bitch.' I said, 'I'm trying to be a lady.' She said it again, so I got up and apologized to the audience, who could hear her, and I said, 'Play it yourself, bitch. You're supposed to be a piano player.' So she played it, and I sang. The audience loved it. They thought it was part of the act! After the show she said, 'Let's stay together.' '' Brown remained with Dinah off and on for close to two years, although like Wynton Kelly and innumerable piano players before her, she and Dinah had frequent fallings-out.

Sometime during the first half of 1961 Dinah recorded again in New York with an orchestra under the direction of Quincy Jones, who in that year was named music director at Mercury Records, a position that, according to friends and associates of Dinah's, he got partly because of Dinah's influence. Jones, however, had not been hanging around waiting for Dinah to get him a job. Since going to Europe with Lionel Hampton in 1957, he'd studied musical composition in Paris, served as musical director at a Paris music studio, and then gone to Stockholm, Sweden, where he served as musical director of *Free and Easy,* an ''opera'' written by the American composer Harold Arlen. The opera had toured Europe in 1959 and 1960, and Jones had enlisted the services of his and Dinah's goddaughter, Patti Austin, as a young member of the company. After the show closed, he'd toured briefly in the United States with his own, eighteen-piece big band before deciding that the cost of supporting eighteen musicians and their familes was too high.

Patti Austin attended that recording session. "It was after I had come back from doing *Free and Easy,* and I was maybe eleven or twelve," she recalls. "I hadn't heard from Dinah for about three years, but I was so involved in my own stuff that I really didn't think about it. She had changed a lot from the last time I'd seen her. Of course, I was older, so I was seeing a lot more than I saw when I was a little child. She was pleased with what I had become, but I'll tell you, there was a jealousy there that was not there when I was a child. It was something I felt from other people, too, not just her. It was just a female thing. That was part of why she seemed different. But she was also drinking a lot. Now, she might have been doing that when I was a kid, but I didn't see it then. Now I knew what the stuff was. She was boozing her brains loose—pink champagne. I remember her coming into the studio and me being there as kind of a surprise for her, and she was really happy to see me, and she hugged me and kissed me. But the drunker she got, the more I felt this vibration of jealousy from her. I'm sure, in retrospect, that it was about my youth—I was just getting ready to be a teenybopper and I had all these possibilities ahead of me. At that point, her career was not yet shaky, and as I recall, that album she recorded with Quincy did quite well, but it was just a little strange. I remember feeling that gaze from Dinah and feeling very uncomfortable and very unhappy and not really, at that point, understanding the basis for it. Then it just really hurt a lot, and I thought to myself, 'Why is she doing this?' I attributed it to the fact that she was getting drunker and drunker with every take. And I remember her coming in the studio and not being able to sing until she had her pink champagne. She sat in a chair and said, 'Where's my pink champagne? Can't sing without my champagne, now.' And Quincy would say, 'Oh, yeah, no problem. Pink champagne coming up. You want a buzz-on? If that's gonna get this performance out of you, great.' And that's what he did. He just sort of played around with it. And she just kind of went out and goofed around and did some takes, and he'd stroke her a little bit and say, 'That's great. Want some more pink champagne? Can we please get this record done?' They got it done. I remember her stumbling out of there, but they got it done. And of course, drunk, sober, upside down, right side up, she sang her ass off.''

Dinah's jealously of Patti Austin may also have been due to the fact that Patti seemed to be doing so much better than Dinah's own kids, about whom she worried constantly. ''She didn't really want them to be in show business,'' says LaRue Manns, ''but they were interested, and so she sent them to dance school, drum school. The eldest one played drums. She had Cozy Cole and Gene Krupa teaching him drums. The youngest one was a dancer and was taking piano lessons. She had Cholly Atkins and Honi Coles teaching him. On occasion, she would have them perform with her at the Apollo or maybe at a theater in Chicago or Philadelphia. She would have them come on as a special attraction once or twice during the time she was performing. At Birdland, she would have the eldest son come up and play drums. But after a while she realized that the team was not going to last. They would bicker among themselves—you didn't do this right, you didn't do that right. She spent a lot of money on it, but she was beginning to know within herself that it wasn't going to work. They didn't pursue it.''

Gordon Austin, Patti's father, was also at that recording session. ''It was just at the beginning of the time when Dinah was going down, and she didn't show up until late, and everybody was uptight. Quincy had some of the finest musicians in the country at this record date, and he would get her at the right time, with the right attitude and the right feeling, when she could sing. And he would take these takes and dub it in with the orchestra in the background, like she was there. They released records that, I think, she didn't even know she'd sung on, because that's how spaced out she was at that time. That's when I started drifting from her—didn't see her anymore after that. I was busy with my family and didn't have time to worry about those things. She'd come up in my mind every now and then, and I'd call her, but she'd be out or something. When I was able to get in touch with her, she'd always have to go—'I got to go, I got to go.' She'd see all these messages that I'd called and she'd call me and ask if everything was all right. I'd tell her, 'Fine,' and then I wouldn't hear anything more.''

In mid-October Dinah was again hospitalized, this time in New York, for four days. She could not rest longer because she was due to play back-to-back engagements at the Apollo Theater and at the 5000 Club in Brooklyn. In between, she got into a lot of trouble. In fact, in the course of one night she threatened a dressmaker with a gun and was arrested and was threatened with charges for having missed a gig. The dressmaker was one Lois Green of Harrisburg, Pennsylvania, who claimed Dinah owed her seven hundred dollars. Green was living in Dinah's apartment at the time, so she didn't have far to go when she tried to collect her money. She chose the wrong time to ask for it, however. It was around 9:00 P.M. on a Friday night when Dinah was supposed to have been appearing at the 5000 Club. Instead, Dinah was at home, having decided she just wasn't up to performing that night and that she'd rather have a few friends in. Ferris Kimbrough explains, ''The reason she didn't show for that gig was that she was disturbed. She had to have a certain amount of rest, a certain amount of sleep. The Apollo Show didn't bring in enough money for her to pay her dressmaker. Now, she explained to me why she didn't pay the dressmaker, but she didn't explain to the dressmaker. And that's who she should have explained it to." Instead, according to Green, Dinah asked Green why she had been telling people she hadn't been paid. Then she asked Green to lend her her car. Green refused, and Dinah waved a gun in her face and threatened to "blow your brains out." Green went to another part of the apartment and stewed for a while. She tried calling the police, but someone in another room was using the phone, and for forty-five minutes she could not get through. Finally, she said, she packed her things, left the apartment, and went to the police station.

Meanwhile, Irwin Steinhauser, brother of the owner of the 5000 Club, arrived with his doctor and two policemen in tow. Seems that the club was jam-packed with an expectant crowd waiting to hear Dinah, and he wanted his doctor to certify that she was really too ill to perform. He'd brought along the policemen, apparently, to forestall possible objections from Dinah. They found Dinah in bed. The party, according to Ferris Kimbrough, had been a dud: "It was unusual for her to have a dud party, but only a few had showed up, and they'd had a drink or something to eat and left. LaRue went bowling, and I went around the corner to the bar." If Kimbrough's recollections are accurate, Steinhauser and his entourage found Dinah alone and in bed and did not feel they could press the demand that Steinhauser's doctor examine her. They were just leaving when Lois Green arrived with two detectives from the 152nd Street police station. It was now about 3:00 A.M. Saturday morning. The detectives searched the apartment but found no gun; nevertheless, on Green's complaint, they took Dinah down to the station for questioning. Dinah put on a red wig, a green beaver coat over a white suit, and a white mink hat for the occasion. She was released on five hundred dollars bail pending a hearing the next day at which Green admitted that she had not actually seen Dinah with a gun, only that she'd seen "an item" under Dinah's negligee, and that she might have called Dinah a "dumb, stupid moron." Later, the charge against Dinah was reduced from felonious assault to third-degree assault.

The story made all the papers. Steinhauser told reporters that when he'd arrived, there were about fifteen people in the apartment and enough empty liquor bottles to account for a two-day party. Says Ferris Kimbrough, "The bottles were there, but they were still full, because there wasn't anybody to drink them."

Whether or not Dinah actually pulled a gun on her dressmaker, she did own a gun. According to LaRue Manns, she had guns around for protection. "That came after Marian Anderson, or someone, was robbed on the highway. We were traveling, and she had a lot of jewelry. Dinah said, 'If we're gonna travel, we need a gun. You carry that little piece. You find somebody that don't look kosher, you pull it and pop it.' There was a gun in the apartment, or somewhere around; if she didn't have it, I had it, or it was in the luggage. But she wasn't any Pistol-Packin' Mama."

In December, Dinah was in Chicago for a recording session for Mercury Records. Quincy Jones was set to direct the session. Jack Wilson, who'd been drafted out of Dinah's entourage several years earlier, had just been discharged from the army. "She called my house in Chicago," says Wilson. "I was surprised she even knew I was out. She wanted me to come to the recording session and I thought I was just going to listen and look. I go there and I'm sitting there, and Quincy Jones is there, and they've got about twenty-five strings and stuff, and the next thing I know she comes over to me and says, 'You play the next number.'

Right out of the blue. She had Patti Brown working with her, a sweet woman and a good pianist. I walk over to Patti and introduce myself and tell her Dinah wants me to play instead of her. Patti is so nice and she goes off. Billy Byers, a guy who had ghostwritten some arrangements for Dinah, asks Patti why she isn't playing on the next number, and she says Dinah asked me to play. He gets mad and tells her to go back and sit down and that she is the piano player on the date. Patti comes back and says to me, 'Hey, I'm sorry, but Quincy and Billy say they want me to play.' So I could dig that. I understood. I got up and walked back and sat in my little seat. Dinah, meanwhile, comes out of the booth and looks at me and says, 'What are you doing sitting there? I told you to go play.' I explained to her what happened. Baby, she got up on the microphone in that recording studio and sounds like the Lord or something coming out. She says, 'Billy Byers and Quincy Jones, I want you to know one thing. This is my record date, and if I want John the Baptist to play, that is who is going to play.' After she said that, Quincy and them didn't say nothing. They were sort of looking like little kids who had been reprimanded. So then I walked over there and sat down at the piano, and we went on and did the tune. It's 'I Wanna Be Loved,' which she had recorded earlier and then re-recorded. I still hear it on the jukeboxes a lot in New York, and I'm pleased that the one number I was on is still around.''

According to Leonard Feather, the only song Dinah ever really stumbled on was recorded at this session. ''Sometimes she would change the words around or get them a little bit screwed up, but it didn't seem to matter. She always made it sound like that was the way it was supposed to be. The only record that I ever heard that she really screwed up was 'I'm Mad About the Boy,' and that was a very sophisticated song. She sings part of a melody a bar too soon or something, and they put it out just the way she did it, and it really sounds weird. So, she obviously didn't know what the song was all about. But that was the only time I heard her really goof up. Generally speaking, she could take almost any song and sort of adjust it to her personality. In the case of the blues, there was no adjustment needed—that was her, right there. That's why she took to those songs of mine—they were just tailor-made for her.''

That record session brought Jack Wilson and Dinah Washington back together. Says Wilson, ''As it turned out, she and Patti Brown were not getting along, so after that I joined her again. This time it was just regular piano, bass, and drums—no seven-piece band. That was in the winter of 1961-62. We left Chicago and went down and played the Saratoga Hotel in Miami Beach, stayed in Miami at the Sir John because the hotels down there were still segregated.''

That recording session in late 1961 was also Dinah's last for Mercury. Around the same time, she signed a contract with Roulette Records, leaving Mercury after fifteen years. ''They weren't helping her do what she wanted to do,'' says Ruth Bowen,'' and she was extremely fond of Morris Levy.'' Despite efforts by Dinah, Arnold Shaw, and probably Quincy Jones, not to mention others, Mercury had refused to see Dinah as an artist who could make the crossover into the mainstream of popular music. The company had consistently marketed her in the black ghettos only, sent its PR releases to the black papers only. Roulette promised her mainstream exposure, and she finally left Mercury, taking arranger Fred Norman, who had often worked with her at Mercury, with her. Arnold Shaw was with Roulette at the time, though he would leave shortly after, and it is likely that he had something to do with the change.

Dinah embarked upon a vigorous recording schedule for Roulette, working primarily with the Don Costa Orchestra, singing a combination of blues and pop. ''She was respon-

sible for my coming out to the Coast,'' says Jack Wilson.
''After I'd joined her again, we went to L.A. to do a record.
It's called *Dinah '62,* and it has 'Where Are You' on it,
which turned out to be a big record for her.'' Benny Carter
did the arrangements, and Buddy Collette and Bill Greene
were also involved in at least one of the recording sessions.
''We were at United, which is one block east of Gower on
Sunset,'' says Greene, ''and we had a session that was called
at seven o'clock. She came in at eight-thirty, and she had
a fifth in her hand that was half gone, and she had a fur
piece dragging on the floor behind her. She said, 'I know
I'm late, but we're going to have only one take on each
song. Two at the most.' We had four songs to do, and I'll
be darned if she wasn't right. We were out of there before
our scheduled time because she was so perfect in her performance. We already had rehearsed the numbers while we
were waiting for her, and I'll never forget that evening. She
was just really powerful in her approach, very sure, positive.
She had a nice vibrato, and her diction was clear, and
everything she did was just perfect.''

As usual, Dinah was not so late that she didn't make
sure some of the musicians got a chance to solo. Says Buddy
Collete, ''Very few artists that I've seen would ever do that,
especially singers. They say, 'Hi, guys, glad you're here,'
you know. Everybody's doing their work, but they're not
getting any play. Dinah would say, 'Hey, wait a minute.
I've got to let Buddy play a solo, I've got to let Jack play
a solo.' And she'd propose these things just before you'd
go into the tune. The tune might be three minutes, but she'd
figure a way to open it up where she could hear all her
favorite people on her own records. She'd sing and then
she'd stand back and sort of let everybody play. It was
almost like a jam session when she recorded. That was very
unusual, because most of the time when you're on a date
with a star, you know who the star is and you're kind of

there to back them up, but with Dinah, she let you know that you were sort of on the same level. She'd make sure that when the record came out, everybody there got a little part, a little share of the glory. That helps when you're working—she'd get you exposed on the record, and your name would be on the album. Naturally, she got a lot of wonderful music that way because the people all got a chance to contribute not just sectionwise but also solowise. I could see that she was so much for musicians. She was closer to musicians, probably, than even Billie Holiday, who loved musicians. Billie was more into liking certain ones, like Lester Young; Dinah surrounded herself with musicians. She picked up something from about every musician she played with, and that was ideal because each person has a different sound. One may play better or higher or faster, but they all have something to say, and Dinah was able to get this out of her players. That's the key to the whole thing: hearing a lot of players, and if you're lucky, you'll like a lot of them because they're all different and you can draw from that. It's like someone that has traveled all over the world and come back with a lot of wisdom and know-how and it's not from any one thing but from a lot of things.

"She was real easy to be with. She was very relaxed and had a lot of stories, kept everybody feeling good. She was one of the guys, but she was still a woman. You felt that she was free and relaxed and anything you wanted to do or say was okay. Sometimes when you work for Lena Horne or Ella Fitzgerald, you are well aware that you're on your best behavior. But Dinah was so regular—she'd tell you some good stories and have the band just rolling on the floor. She was earthy. You probably couldn't have frightened her with any kind of story, and she told some good ones herself. She had a freedom there, and it came off in her music."

For Jack Wilson, that record date opened up new career

possibilities. "I met Gerald Wilson and Buddy Collette on that record date, and Gerald told me he had a big band that he was getting together, and if I wanted to stay in California, he'd like me to join his band." A few months later, Wilson did leave Dinah for the West Coast. There were no hard feelings. Dinah wished him well.

Dinah recorded a great deal, mostly in New York, for Roulette. Some of her songs reached the top hundred on the charts, but they were far from being in the top ten, and as Patti Austin recalls, that affected Dinah's bookings on the road. "The whole industry had changed. Before that, she could get booked almost anywhere because she was Dinah Washington, hit record or no hit record. Now it was like, what was your last hit? Well, I'm sorry, you're not gonna draw in the clubs because Gloria Lynne over here has ten hit records, that's who everybody wants to hear."

Ironically, it was Dinah who had given Gloria Lynne one of her first big breaks. Says Ruth Bowen, "I remember once she called me. She was at the Apollo Theater, and there was a young lady whose talent she admired, Gloria Lynne. Dinah said, 'I think I'm gonna get sick Saturday morning. You wait until the last minute before you call Bobby Schiffman, because it'll be too late for him to find anybody, and you tell him you got somebody and put Gloria Lynne in there.' It worked. She even had some gowns in the dressing room for Gloria to wear, so she would look nice. Dinah loved for everybody to look nice. Gloria went on. Bobby hit the ceiling, of course, but there was nothing he could do because he couldn't find anybody. And Gloria tore the house down. By the third show, Dinah got well. She said, 'Now, let's not overdo it.' "

It was indeed all about hit records now, and it had been some time since Dinah had had a record in the top ten. In fact, "Tears and Laughter," which entered the charts on

February 5, 1962, was, at number ten, Dinah's last top-ten record. All subsequent releases that made the charts were only in the top twenty. And when "it" wasn't about records, it was about exposure on TV. Back in 1953, Dinah could have a hit with a wryly comical song called "TV Is the Thing (This Year)," which expressed the opinion of many people that television was a passing fad that wouldn't last. Less than twenty years later, TV was the thing, period, and old-timers like Dinah had a hard time adjusting to lip-syncing for the cameras. "My last memory of her was, I think, seeing her on *American Bandstand*," says Patti Austin. "She was singing the last record she made with Brook Benton—I think it was *Broken Hearted Melody*—and she went on and lip-synced the record. At that time I hadn't seen her in about two years, and she never, ever, matched the record—not once did my girl hit the lyrics—and I remember being so disillusioned. This is my hero, and she can't even lip-sync her own record! How long could it take to do this—three times in front of a mirror? I remembered her being very professional all the time, and that really disillusioned me, because by that time I was making my own records and lip-syncing my own records. It was like, Come on, you're my godmother, don't do this in public!"

Young Patti Austin, who'd practically grown up lip-syncing for television, did not understand how hard it was for a performer who'd sung live for thirty years to do so. The lack of spontaneity was just not Dinah's style. She hated "mouthing," as she called it, and knew that she did it badly. "I never sing a song the same way twice. The lyrics always change a bit. There's always a fluff," she had confessed to a Toronto reporter in 1959. Patti Austin's awareness, now, of how the changes in the music industry affected Dinah Washington is based on the knowledge accumulated during her own long career in the music industry. She was not close to Dinah Washington at this time. "We just stopped hearing from her. I think she felt that she had done all she could do, which she did—and more. And all of it was above and beyond the call of duty, and if it had not been for her, I would not be doing any of what I am doing now. Maybe it would have happened from somewhere else, but she was the reason that I am in the industry.''

Dinah still had fans galore and was as welcome as ever in the nitty-gritty places whose audiences had supported her all her performing career. She still felt most comfortable in these clubs, for she knew what the audiences wanted and was more than happy to give it to them. To the end of her career, she continued to sing Leonard Feather's ''Long John Blues'' in as lowdown a manner as possible, rolling her big eyes in a way that left little to the imagination. She continued also to regard whatever club she was in, big or small, like her own living room (or like her ''court'') and to berate those who did not pay her sufficient obeisance. It didn't faze her that the Frolic in Revere, Massachusetts, seated 450 patrons. Nobody was going to frolic when Dinah Washington was onstage. She'd fix the offending table with her most frightening evil gal stare and bark, ''Shut up,'' without missing a beat in her song. Trouble was, the down-home clubs were fast disappearing, victims of television, which was having a marked effect on American nightlife, or the lack thereof, by then. They were victims, too, of the burgeoning record business—why pay to go to hear a singer at a club when you could sit in your own living room and play the hi-fi? Finally, they were victims of integration: Slowly, but noticeably, at least in the North, white clubs were opening their stage doors and their front doors to blacks, and given a choice, many blacks preferred to exercise their new freedom than to remain loyal to clubs that had served them in the days when they had no choice. Most of the black clubs that remained open were not any more capable of paying Dinah big money than they had been

before, and she still had to work more one-nighters in more
out-of-the way places than most stars of her caliber just to
pay expenses.

"She always had a large entourage," says Ruth Bowen.
"Sometimes she'd just put them on her payroll because she
liked to have them around. A lot of times her payroll was
more than she earned. There was Ann Littles [who func-
tioned as Dinah's road manager and general factotum], the
musicians, a valet, a hairdresser, a seamstress sometimes,
LaRue, sometimes a chauffeur. At one time she decided she
wanted to have her own plane, and she bought this De-
Havilland Dove. I can't remember who she bought it from.
The pilot or somebody owned this damn plane. I think we
met him in Birdland. He said, 'You wanna buy a plane?'
And she said, 'Yes,' and she hounded me to death to buy
this plane. We didn't have a dime to buy it with, but we
got it. Dinah would borrow money from anybody. She'd
call all over—"Send me some money." She had good
relationships with a lot of guys all over.

"So, she bought the plane, and she had the pilot round-
the-clock and drove the pilot absolutely insane. She'd be
going over Ohio or somewhere, going to Illinois, and she'd
say, 'Oh, I got a friend living down there, let's go down
and see him.' When she was coming back from an engagement, she'd come down and buzz my house before
going to the airport. She was a fun person.

"The plane crashed. We were sending her to Las Vegas,
and we had the Dells and some of the musicians, and Lola
Falana, who she discovered and brought out. A lot of people
think that Sammy Davis, Jr., was responsible for first bringing Lola from Philadelphia, but it was Dinah. And she had
them going by the private plane—she was going to go
later—and the darn thing crashed. Nobody was injured,
thank goodness, but that was the end of the plane. It was
like a toy to Dinah."

Dinah was profligate and proud of it. LaRue remembers her saying, often, "I'm gonna have everything I want, the best there is." Since she was always lending money to other people, she had no compunction about borrowing it back, or borrowing from others. She borrowed often from Joe Glaser, though she used her furs as collateral. "He had a storeroom," says LaRue Manns. "I'd put the furs in and she'd borrow the money and use the money. Come time when it got cold, she'd go out on a date and make the money and she'd pay the money and get the things back. If she needed a coat to wear to something, all I had to do was go down and say, 'Mr. Glaser, Dinah's going to such-and-such a place, she needs one coat.' He'd say, 'Hey, somebody, go down there and get Dinah's coat.' I mean, it was one of those things, so it wasn't like they were in hock. We knew a lot of the elite chicks who were going to certain pawn shops and pawning their furs, because furs were the thing at that time. They'd take the money and use it, and then, come fall, they'd get the money back and get the furs out."

By the end of 1962, however, Dinah's getting and spending were not quite so casual or carefree. Checks she wrote for services started bouncing. Irving Ashby, who had once been a guitarist with Nat King Cole and his Trio, remembers, "I was a copyist with Ernie Freeman, the arranger. We went up to San Francisco one time to do about twelve or fourteen tunes for a show she was opening in New York. He's doing all these charts, and I'm sitting down the hall in another room in the hotel separating the charts and copying them. Around the clock we're just writing, writing, writing music. We got it done under the deadline, and he put his bill in, and she paid him. This was, maybe, on a Saturday. We come back down to L.A. and go to the bank on Monday, and we find that she's stopped payment on the check. It was for about eight hundred bucks. We never did get paid."

Being in debt did not, however, stop Dinah from spending extravagantly when she wanted to, which was often. LaRue Manns recalls, "That jeweler, George Ungar, would tell her, 'You're a star, you need to have this, you need to have that.' And that just built her ego, because if he told her something looked good on her and that she should have it, she would go to the limits to get it. He got an awful lot of business out of her, even up until the day she died."

Such ego boosts were fleeting, however, and very expensive. If anything, they contributed to Dinah's downward financial spiral, which in turn fed her downward emotional spiral. By 1962 altercations with her audiences, charges of disorderly conduct, and missed gigs were becoming a habit, and consistently making the papers. "A lot of the time she just didn't feel up to performing," says Manns. "She was taking those pills, and her voice began to come and go, and she couldn't hit the notes like she wanted to. And then when she knew she wasn't singing well, when she couldn't go out and do well, then she would drink very heavily. And if somebody said something to her, then she'd get nasty. I'd say, 'Well, baby, it's time to go home,' and she'd get in the car and we'd go home. Then she'd roam around all night, and you had to sit up with her and play cards with her, watch television, or talk about rambling things. It was a trying time."

In Winston-Salem, North Carolina, she was charged with having walked out of a show at the Memorial Coliseum. Dinah's attorney countercharged that she had chartered a plane in order to make the date and that when she had arrived, just a bit late, she'd been told she was not scheduled to go on for a couple of hours. The attorney, A. Allen Saunders, also charged that the promoters had failed to live up to their contract in terms of advance payment because a check they had sent had been returned by the bank. In Baltimore, Dinah was charged with disorderly conduct and of consuming alcoholic beverages after hours at a place called the Comedy Club, where she was performing. A judge dropped the charges because she had her professional standing to consider. In November, Dinah pulled out of an engagement at Pep's in Philadelphia. Jack Wilson remembers, "She and the club owner had had run-ins before. We drove down to Philadelphia from New York and we're setting up the band up on the stand, and what should happen but the club owner and Dinah got into it, and Dinah came up and told us to pack up. The joint was full, and we packed up and left. She wasn't going to work for this cat." Pat Patterson, local representative of AGVA, the American Guild of Variety Artists, advised Dinah to work out the week, but she ignored him. In Pittsburgh, John Bertera, owner of Holiday House, refused to pay her because of her "unprofessional manner," charging that she had "continuously harassed patrons" and made anti-Semitic remarks, making it necessary for the house to refund cover charges to dissatisfied customers. As a member of the AGVA, whose representatives were in on nearly all these cases, Dinah got her dues' worth from the guild during this period, if not before, or later.

The adverse publicity didn't bother Dinah. "For a while there, it seemed like everything was wrong," says Ruth Bowen. "But Dinah always figured, no matter what, good or bad, get publicity. She'd say, 'Did they spell my name right?' Dinah would create press, one way or another." It is likely that her announcement to members of the press that she wanted a mink toilet seat for Christmas was a combination of milking the publicity she was getting and thumbing her nose at those who were trying to bring her down. Whatever her reasons, she got her mink toilet seats. "Someone gave them to her," says Bowen. "I think it was Morris Levy. No, it might have been the musical director at Universal. Anyway, they were a gift. She said she wanted them and they gave them to her. Dinah believed that everybody needed a piece of mink."

But the stress of all the problems and bad publicity aggravated her already deteriorating mental and physical condition, which in turn caused her to rely more heavily on chemical solutions. By the time she returned home to New York to spend the December holidays with the boys, LaRue was so worried that she questioned Dinah's doctor about his apparent willingness to give Dinah medication anytime she wanted it. "I said, 'Doctor, you keep coming every time she calls—she'll call you three times a day and you'll come by and say you gave her a shot. She should rest.' He says, 'I don't give her medication every time she asks, even though she may say so. She's taking prescription medicine I'm not familiar with (this was another doctor, not the same one who gave her the mercury injections). She just has to let it go out of her system. But her system is just about gone. She's almost living on borrowed time because her system is so worn out from taking pills to make her perk up, pills to make her lose weight, pills to make her put weight on, pills to take the water off, pills to go to the bathroom.' Her resistance was just gone."

But Dinah couldn't stop. After spending the Christmas holidays in New York, she went back on the road and in Detroit came down with pneumonia, not to mention a recurrence of her chronic case of needing someone to lean on. This time, Dick "Night Train" Lane appeared to fill the prescription.

"THE first time I met Dinah was [1952] my rookie year
playing with the [Los Angeles] Rams," says former half-
back Dick "Night Train" Lane. "Billy Eckstine took me
to see her at the Tiffany Club on Eighth Street. I met Billy
when I was in the service in 1948. He saw me standing
outside the theater where he was playing and gave me tickets
to the show. In 1952, I met him again at one of the clubs
in L.A., where Nellie Lutcher was singing, I think. I reminded him of what he did for me when I was just a poor
soldier, and he said, 'Let's go by the Tiffany and see Gene
Gibson and Damita Joe.' Dinah was there when we came
in, and Billy introduced me to Dinah. I said to her, 'You
don't know. My wife don't do nothing but sit in the corner
all day and play your records.'

"The next time I saw her was about a year later. We
were at some birthday party and she says, 'I know you,'
and I said, 'Yeah, football player,' and she says, 'Oh.' The
next year, the end of the '53 season, I got traded to Chicago,
which is her home, and we would run across each other
frequently. I had a girlfriend who was married to Eddie
'Rochester' Anderson's son, Jerry, and Jerry invited me to
a party he was giving for Dinah one night. Some of her

stepbrothers were there, and we sat around and talked, and Dinah, she gets kind of like she wants to take over the show. She starts dealing out them old bad vibes. I say, 'Girl, you know what? If I was your old man, I'd put half my fist down your throat, talking like that.' She says, 'You know who you're talking to?' I said, 'I don't really give a . . . hoot.' She had a drink in her hand, and she poured this drink on me. And I reached out and grabbed her and—we were on the twenty-second floor—and was going to throw her off the twenty-second floor. Everybody is screaming and hollering, 'Oh, don't throw her out that window!' I didn't. I just told Jerry, 'I appreciate the hospitality, and I'm going.' I told Dinah, 'You oughta try and clean up your mouth.' She gives me a look and says something like, 'He can't take it.' I went and got the elevator and went home.

"The next time I saw her was in Cleveland, where we went to play an exhibition game. The guys wanted to go down to this club and catch Dinah's first show. Me and two other guys go down there, and we're standing back by this pillar. The night before, she'd been in some after-hours joint that had gotten raided, and when she opened up the show, she said, 'I guess everybody heard about me being in jail last night. These cats were just shooting craps, and I was having a little fun with my fans.' That's the way she opened up the show. Then she says, 'Yeah, I think there's one of them standing over by that pillar.' So, I step out from the pillar. She says, 'Oh, no, it's the football player!' She never had forgotten me. From then on, we became real palsy-walsy and crossed paths from time to time.

"Then I got traded to Detroit, and we met up again at the house of a friend. She asked me what I was doing, and I told her I had a little restaurant, Night Train Lane's El Taco Stop. Next time she played Detroit, she called me one night. She asked for me, and the guy who answered said I was busy. She said, 'Well, tell him I want some food.' She

ordered some food, and I guess she thought I was going to
bring it. I sent my helper. The next night she called again,
and this time she insisted that I bring it.

"So I brought the food, and she was eating, and coughing. I said, 'Girl, you got a bad cough. You ought to see
a doctor.' She said it was the place—they leave the door
open and it gets cold, then they turn the heat up and it gets
hot. I gave her my home phone number and told her to call
me anytime she wanted. She called the same night, and it
turned out she was staying at the Hollander, a little motel
right around the corner from me. I said, 'Girl, what do you
want?' She said, 'I want to talk.'

"So, I went around. She has some girl over from Chicago doing her toenails and stuff and she's still coughing.
I said, 'Why don't you call a doctor? You don't look too
well. You didn't look too well at the club.' She admitted
that she was really feeling bad. Then I offered to take her
back to my place and call my doctor. I said to her, 'You
can bring your maid or whoever you want to.' So after I
get her over to my place, I call my doctor. He comes over
and he says she has pneumonia. He wants her to go to the
hospital, but she doesn't want to go to the hospital. So I
go in and say, 'You gotta go to the hospital, you can't die
here.' She's cracking up. She says, 'He's funny, doctor.'
I say, 'Yeah, I'm fat, but I ain't funny.' We end up taking
her to a little clinic nearby, my doctor knows the physician
on duty, and the physician says she's got to get to bed,
she's got pneumonia, she shouldn't work for a week or two.

"So, we go back to my house, and I put her to bed.
She stays at my place, and it gives us a chance to talk. I'm
single, I had no wife. I had a seven-room house, rented the
bottom out, but still had a lot of room upstairs. So we talked,
and I really didn't realize how lonely she was and how much
she did to make people love her.

"She was always trying to please her mother. She felt

that her mother didn't love her, and she thought that if her mother would love her, then everybody else would—her friends she grew up with, all the other people. Those stresses came early in her life, and she just felt that there was nothing she could do to please her mother.''

Listening to Dinah talk, Lane realized that they had a lot in common. ''It was something like me—I've been out on my own since I was fifteen years old. You learn to kind of keep people at arm's length—even those that you feel you need to get close to, you kind of set yourself off from. So, we were two alike, and we were sitting there laughing and saying, yeah, we both this, that, and the other.

''About the seventh day, she says, 'Would you do something for me? I want you to take over my business.' I said, 'Oh, come on.' She said, 'You do pretty well in your business. From all indications, and from what the guys around here tell me, you're pretty much your own man.' I said, 'Yeah, I've been that for a long time, make my own decisions. I don't know what you're leading up to, but I'm not a kid and nobody dangles me around.' She laughed.

''So, I nursed her back to health and she brought a girl from California in one day, and I come in, and she says to the girl, 'I want you to cook for Train. He needs a cook down there in his place, and I'm taking over his place.' I said, 'Wait a minute, hold on.'

''Meanwhile, Ruth Bowen has flown in. Her husband, Billy Bowen, and I were good friends—he played with the Ink Spots. Dinah and Ruth are talking about what they're going to do, and Ruth wants some decisions. I tell her, 'No, I don't think you should leave here. You tell the people in Vegas that you are too ill to work. You've been neglecting this for a long time. They'll understand. The people at the Flame Bar [in Detroit] will understand that you'll make up the week when you can.' I end up going to the people at the Flame Bar and telling them myself, and so I began to get a little bit involved in her business.

"While she was recuperating, she began to teach me about it, and I asked about this, and I asked about that, and we did that for quite some time. Finally, when I felt she was able to go out to Vegas—she was to do four weeks—I told her she should go. She wanted me to go with her. I said no. So, she goes out to Vegas, but meanwhile, anyone who is calling her, she's telling them they've got to talk to me. And she's calling me every day and giving me her numbers, where she's going to be.

"Next thing I know, I get a call from a reporter. She told Ruth she was going to marry me, and Ruth told the press. I call Dinah and cuss her out. I tell her, 'You retract all that stuff.' But Dinah is a very smart lady. She knows who my best friend is, because we've been talking. She calls him—Chauncey Estridge, he's an attorney—and she says, 'You tell him it's a good deal, and I'll obey him and I'll do this and I'll do that.' He calls me up and says, 'I've got two tickets and I'm coming over and we're going to Vegas to talk to this girl.' Meanwhile, all these society reporters are calling me to ask, 'Is it true you and Dinah are getting married?' And all my buddies are calling to say, 'I saw in the paper this morning . . .'

"Then she called. 'I know you're mad,' she says. I say, 'Yeah, I'm mad. I told you before I'm not one of those little kids you play with.' She says, 'If you come out, and you don't want to go through with it, you don't have to.' I said okay. This was about February 1963. I was dating a gal and I'd had a little run-in with her, and I guess that made up my mind. So I took a plane out to Vegas. My attorney is already there. I say, 'What are you doing here in Vegas?' He says, 'I'm going to be your best man.' I said, 'Lord, have mercy!'

"She's got an appointment for me at the haberdashers'. I'm thinking I've heard about Las Vegas marriages, that they're not worth the paper they're on. Why should I be worried? Meanwhile, the guys that owned the Thunderbird are telling me how much they love her and how glad they are that I nursed her back to health and how she needs somebody to take care of her. And I get a chance to talk to her and I tell her, 'I'm not a baby. I do not play games. If you've got somebody you're taking care of—if I find out about it, that's the end. I've heard about all your involvements and all the people you give money to. I don't need that. I make my own money, and that way I stay away from problems.' The next thing I knew, I was married.''

Justice of the Peace Tom Pursel performed the ceremony in the Little Church of the West, on July 2, 1963. Ruth Bowen was in attendance. LaRue was not because she was ill with an ulcer at the time. ''And shortly after that, I had to go into the hospital to have an ulcer operation. Before that, I had been in the hospital for another operation, and Dinah paid for that, you know. She was just so good to me in many ways.''

Dick Lane soon found out that Dinah was being good to a lot of people. ''She was paying some policeman's car note in Chicago and some house rental for somebody else who was down. She didn't forget the people who were down in the real hard times. She loved Martin Luther King. They were very close, and she often talked with him. I guess somewhere along the line they [FBI] tried to tie her in as a lover or something. She always sent him money and always did what he wanted her to do. [In 1960 Dinah had urged a ban on the sale of her records in southern states that approved segregation.] She had a good heart, and a good memory, she was just a very poor businesswoman.

''Things began moving that year. I took over the business, started checking [things] out. When the season started, I had to get on the plane on Mondays and go to New York, check this out, check that out. The plane she bought was impounded somewhere. She bought Robbie Cummings's plane and then had it shipped to Virginia. Then there was the kids' school—at this time they were in Windsor Mountain School in Massachusetts, where my foster daughter was, and they couldn't start the fall semester until the bills were paid. I got ahold of Ruth in New York and said, 'Look, I'm gonna send this money because I believe in the kids getting their education, but I want to be reimbursed.' I didn't know what I'd gotten into—I was out twelve thousand dollars before I could even sneeze. There were just a hundred and one things.''

Dinah was equally busy. For the first time in years she was happy and feeling hopeful about the future. She was moving to Detroit, and LaRue Manns, for one, realized that this was a major step. ''Her famous words, and anyone who ever knew Dinah even a little had heard them, were, 'I would never leave New York to go to heaven,' '' says Manns. ''But then she met Night Train, and fell in love, and suddenly she's talking about moving to Detroit. I said, 'But Dinah, you said you would never leave New York to go to heaven.' She said, 'Well, maybe *I have met* heaven.'

''And it wasn't long after they got married that she decided she was going to settle there. She was going to open an office [of Queen Artists Corp.] there and move me out there to handle the business from there and leave Ruthie here to handle this office. Ruthie's husband was still living then, so with me not having a husband at that time, I could go. So I said, 'I don't know whether I want to live in Detroit or not.' She said, 'Oh, yeah, you know a lot of people here, you'll get along just fine. We'll still have a good time.' And, oh, I guess about a month after that she called and asked us to call the packers in and move out. We had a housekeeper, and she took the housekeeper out to Detroit with her. So much stuff got stored away.''

Dinah was establishing herself in Detroit, helping to found a civic group called the Ballantine Belles with a longtime friend named Bea Buck. ''She began to try to be a wife as well as a star and a businesswoman," says LaRue Manns. "She was getting involved in [Lane's] restaurant —giving new menus and fixing it up. She liked that. And the restaurant was crowded every day because people knew that she was going to be there, and they wanted to come and shake her hand and get her autograph."

Her career was picking up. She performed with Duke Ellington and his orchestra at the Michigan State Fair and with the Count Basie Orchestra at the Ravinia Park Festival in Chicago, as well as more dates in hotels and better clubs. Meanwhile, she was still recording for Roulette, and because she had stopped drinking heavily after her marriage to Lane, she felt more like doing it all.

Although Dinah was not drinking as heavily, she still kept cases of brandy in the house. And she still took all those pills. "She had this thing about her weight," says Night Train Lane. "She had these pills and these syringes for taking off the water. She'd got with some pharmacy back there [in New York], and she'd take syringes and drain off the excess water. How she drained it, I don't know, but she could lose twenty to thirty pounds overnight. I felt at times, when she drank a lot of brandy and didn't have a rest, she really blew up. She had a pill for everything. I flushed them down the toilet. The other day, I realize—I'm taking all these herbs and things—I'm taking about as many pills as she was." But Dinah's pills were not harmless "herbs."

"They were prescription medicines," says Gordon Austin, who saw her once during this time. "She'd gotten a little bit heavier, and she wasn't sleeping well. She had to take two or three pills every hour on the hour, and she had this pill box with the date and time she was supposed to take them."

Dinah's continued concern about her weight is not hard to understand, but why wasn't she sleeping well? Some people suggest that her marriage to Lane might not have been quite as rosy as it was publicly portrayed.

LaRue Manns recalls, "The last conversation Dinah and I had, she told me that when they got married, Night Train was at the end of his career—the team was going to give him up because of his age, I think, and he had a bad knee or something. After they got married, the club kept him for another year. This would boost the team if one of their top stars married a star. People would come out to see if Dinah was going to be there. It was a boost for both of them."

Evelyn Parker concurs. Having grown up in Detroit, she remembers Lane when he played for Miller High School. "He didn't have a very good reputation. There was some scandal about drug use among the players." While she did not know him personally, she had kept up with her friends in Detroit and was aware of the talk. "He wasn't doing well at all when he married her. I think he was using her. But I guess her needs were very heavy at the time."

Lane agrees that his marriage to Dinah gave him "some wonderful moments." "All of the team, and Bill Ford and his wife, came out when Dinah performed here in Detroit and sat through three shows. In the ghetto—unbelievable. I'm sitting there looking at that man, he's worth six hundred and fifty million dollars. His wife wants to see another show, and he sits there and catches another show. William Clay Ford. They would sit backstage and talk, and they came over to the house. It was unbelievable how she could take kings and bring them under her spell; and she could take the tramp out there in the street and the prostitute and do the same thing."

In early December, Dinah played Basin Street in Los Angeles. Leonard Feather, who had moved to the West Coast in 1960 and had not seen her for several years, took his wife to see her. "Just as my wife walked in the door, she was singing the first line of 'Blowtop Blues,' which goes, 'I got bad news, baby, and you're the first to know.' Then there was a little pause before she did the last part, and during that pause she looked at me and said, 'Would you believe a white man wrote this song?' and went on with the song. I'll always remember that. I went to the dressing room afterward and kissed her and thanked her, and everything was very emotional. I had no idea that she was going to die so soon, because she was not ill. She just wasn't taking care of herself.''

Jack Wilson, who had left Dinah about a year earlier to join Gerald Wilson's orchestra, went to see her closing night. ''I had my wife with me, who was pregnant with my daughter at the time. She called me up on the stage and told everybody in the audience that I used to work with her but that she couldn't afford me anymore, which was of course not true, but it was very gracious of her to say it. We played together. I did a couple numbers with her and the band, and it was all very beautiful. She was radiant, she was beaming. I had never seen her so happy. I said, 'Well, how're you doin'?' And she said, 'I'm doing fine. Me and Night Train have this business in Detroit . . .' They had franchised some fast-food restaurants. They had all these plans. She had finally married a man who wasn't Mr. Dinah Washington and she could be a woman, you know, and relax.''

Dinah had arranged to relax with her family for a full three weeks that December. Her next performance was not until New Year's Eve at a charity ball in Detroit, where she would be billed ''Dinah Sings with Strings.'' In the interim she was going to do Christmas up proud.

LaRue Manns remembers, ''I was going to spend the Christmas holidays with her. She'd called and she'd bought all these Christmas presents. Christmas was her time of year. She liked birthdays and she liked Christmas. She would just go all-out—there was no limit to how much she would

spend—and she didn't care if she took the next six months
to pay for it.'' After that telephone conversation, Manns
was also eager to be with Dinah because Dinah had told
her that her marriage to Night Train Lane was not quite as
heaven-made as it appeared. ''She'd told me—and she had
an eagle eye—that she thought he was still seeing someone else after the few months of marriage, and she felt
that it was his old girlfriend.'' It was during that same
telephone conversation that Dinah told Manns she felt that
perhaps Lane had used her to extend his football career.
Manns wanted to get out there and see for herself what was
going on.

While Dinah was indeed troubled by her suspicions that
Night Train was still seeing his former girlfriend, nothing
could keep Dinah down at Christmastime. She'd spent days
decorating the house at 4002 Buena Vista Street, using
decorations she'd had shipped in from New York. She'd
bought a pinkish-white artificial tree that reached almost to
the ceiling, and she spent part of the day of December 13
decorating it. She also went shopping. Someone said that
in just one store she spent more than $2,400 for gifts and
decorations. She bought an electric toothbrush for Night
Train, and custom-made sweaters for him and the boys. She
bought gifts for her cooks and housekeepers and for friends
across the country. She wrapped them all herself, taping
funny notes on some of them, notes like ''Yeah, I know
you thought I'd forgotten you, but who could forget a face
like yours?'' and ''You stole enough money to buy your
own damn gift, but I thought I'd send you something anyway,'' ''Take this and wear it with pride, 'cause, honey,
you've got something you really ought to hide!'' ''This is
the season to be jolly . . . and I would be—if I didn't know
so many people like you!'' Nothing could keep her spirits
down at Christmas, and this Christmas she felt especially
happy. Her husband might be stepping out on her, but that

didn't mean he would continue. Dinah wasn't a stranger to unfinished business between men and their former women, or women and their former men. She may have been willing to give him some leeway for a while, before she put a stop to it. Dinah was a fighter, and in Night Train she believed that she'd found a man worth fighting for. He was a real man, a take-charge man, and a man she believed really cared about her children and was prepared to be a father to them. "She wanted a strong man for the kids," says Manns, "because they were teenagers and at least one of them was beginning to go a little rocky—going to wild parties and losing his coat and jewelry and stuff." Lane felt that the major problem was that Dinah was away from them so much. "I told her we were going to make amends."

"My last game of the season, we were going to play in Chicago," says Lane. "We were going to meet the kids at the airport when they came in from Windsor Mountain, and then go to Chicago and take Mama Jones shopping for a little bit and spend a few days with her mother right before Christmas.

"So I come in from practice and we were due at the airport in ten, fifteen minutes to pick up the kids, and then we were going to go on to Chicago. But she says, 'Baby, you go pick them up, and let's go in the morning.' I'm thinking I could have saved all this airfare, because we could have gone with the team, and I'm mad about that now. But she had a way. She kissed me on the cheek and said, 'Go pick up the kids, and I promise you, we'll go first thing in the morning.' I said, 'Okay.' She sounded so tired, but I really didn't notice it. I was kind of like a kid, too, because I was so enthused about us making it this far, because I thought it wouldn't last two minutes, and it was getting better and better every day.

"So, I went and picked up the kids and brought them home and we all had dinner. The kids talked with me about what they were doing at school. Then I said, 'I gotta go to bed.' I could hear Dinah out in the kitchen talking with the maid and the cook, Mama Harris, a lady she'd brought in from L.A. I took a shower and went to bed. The TV woke me up—probably about three, four o'clock in the morning. It had been about eleven o'clock when I went to bed. I decide to turn the TV off, and I start to crawl out my side of the bed, and I put my foot down right on her. I said, 'Dinah? What you doin' down there, girl?' and I picked her up, and she went 'Aaah,' like that. It was the last breath she took. I should have called EMS or something right away, but I went and called her doctor. He said, 'What's the matter?' I said, 'I can't wake her up.' So he rushed over as fast as he could—it was snowing hard. He gave her a shot to try to revive her, but she was gone. When the doctor said she was dead, I didn't believe him. It was just something that went over me that was just unbelievable.''

No one could believe it. LaRue learned the news from a neighbor. ''I was awakened at six o'clock in the morning. Ruthie heard it first, and she called my neighbor to come over and tell me so that I wouldn't be by myself when I heard. I just couldn't believe it. 'Not Dinah,' I said, 'I just talked to her. We're going out there for Christmas.' But they told me to turn the radio on, and I heard it. Then we had to call her mother, and she didn't believe it either. She said, 'Dinah be here in a few minutes. I'm fixing breakfast.'

''As the day went on, it finally began to hit me. I kept thinking that if I'd been out there . . . I had just had the doctor send out a new order of pills and they had just arrived. [According to Detroit police, there was no pharmacy name on the pill bottle.] When I got there [to Detroit] the next evening, we found the pill bottle and figured out how many were missing. It wasn't that many—she hadn't taken an overdose. The other orders hadn't been touched. But if I'd been there, I would have been sitting in the room with her, watching television and watching her. That is what I used to do, sit up half the night with her if I knew she was in that mood and had taken sleeping pills."

Patti Austin says, "I remember hearing about it and having absolutely no reaction at all. I was just numb. I didn't cry. I didn't laugh. I didn't feel anything. It took me about two years to finally cry about it. Actually, it took me two years to believe it. I just kept expecting the phone to ring and hearing her on the other end."

Slappy White was in Baltimore, on his way to the race-track, when he heard the news on the radio. "My own money is short, so I go to the racetrack and maybe I can make a buck. I pull into the racetrack and I cut the radio on, and the news flash comes on saying Dinah Washington has just died. Boy, that hit me. Now I've got to get to the funeral, you know, but I don't have any money. There's no radio at the racetrack, so I'm the only one who knows Dinah's dead, and everybody I tell, they don't believe me anyway, because they say I just want to borrow money. I finally manage to borrow the money to get to Chicago for the funeral. I don't know how I'm going to get back."

Redd Foxx's reaction to the news of Dinah's death was simpler: "I don't blame her; I'd have killed myself, too." He also made plans to attend the funeral.

The music industry reacted as well. Immediately, the airwaves were filled with Dinah's songs—"I Wanna Be Loved," "Teach Me Tonight," "This Bitter Earth." Several black and pop radio stations suspended regular programming for a twenty-four-hour period and played recordings she'd made famous. Record stores, inundated by calls, hastily reordered Dinah's records.

There was no question that Dinah would be buried in Chicago. "That's the town where they've got some real honest-to-goodness, pig-feet-eating 'soul' folk . . . my kind of people," she would say. She often reminded her family that she wanted to be buried there: "When the Queen quits the scene, don't be sending me back home to Tuscaloosa; send the Queen back to the Windy City and lay her out like she's supposed to be!"

There was a memorial service in Detroit first. Dinah's old friend the Reverend C. L. Franklin conducted the service. Thirty-thousand people stood in line for hours in sub-zero weather to file by the open casket and pay their last tribute to the Queen, who was dressed in a yellow chiffon dress, rhinestone-studded shoes, a white mink stole, and a tiara. Then, Dinah's body was taken to Chicago for the funeral at Saint Luke's Baptist Church, where she had sung gospel and played the piano as a child, and where thousands more of her fans braved the frigid weather to see her. The crowds were so dense that police put into effect an emergency traffic control plan. About three thousand managed to get into the church, including the Martin Singers, Mahalia Jackson, Ella Fitzgerald, and Brook Benton, assorted family, ex-family, quasi-family, and ex-quasi-family members. About three thousand more remained outside.

Slappy White was one of the pallbearers. "Me, Redd Foxx, Dick Gregory, and a couple of singers called the Allegros, a singing group that did background on some of her albums. So we go to pick up this big bronze casket. Now, we have seen President Kennedy's funeral and those soldiers picked up his casket like it was nothing, so we think we can do it. Boy, when we picked that casket up and pulled it out of the hearse, it was so heavy coming out of the hearse, I called to some guy to help. I say, 'Hey, buddy, come here a minute and help me with this thing.' A guy says, 'He ain't no pallbearer.' I say, 'He's a pallbearer's helper.' I couldn't hold that big old casket. We carry the casket into the church, one of those old churches she went to during the days she was with her family. We go up a lot of steps. So finally we get to the top of the steps and we're going down the aisle and we put the casket in front of the altar. Redd Foxx tells a guy, 'Listen, pal, you better kind of look in there first before you open it up, because Dinah might be lying on her side. We had a hard time getting that casket up them steps.'

"So now we're in the funeral, and everybody's sitting there, including about five ex-husbands. And there's a lot of show people there, and we'd been drinking and having a good time, that's the type of funeral it was. And everybody has something to say about Dinah, and we stay so long in the church that it's dark by the time we go to the cemetery."

Joe Glaser provided twenty-five Cadillac limousines, and there were about one hundred cars in the funeral procession. Someone had suggested that the casket be flown to Burr Oak Cemetery in a helicopter from which little girls would drop rose petals on the city, but the family decided that would be too showy.

"At the cemetery it was so dark that they had to shine the car headlights on the grave, and the grave has a big old top on it because it's snowing," says White. "We get the casket over on top of the grave, and they press the button for the casket to go down, but it's about seventeen below zero and the thing is frozen. So the undertaker says the mechanics have to come and fix the belt so the casket will go down, and we all have to leave her there on top of the grave." As a matter of fact, that is the way Dinah would have wanted it. Less than a month earlier, she had watched President Kennedy's funeral on television. She told a friend, "You know something, I stood the whole thing pretty well as long as they were carrying his body from place to place, but it really got to me when they got his body to the cemetery and got ready to put his casket in the ground. That was a fine, pretty man about to be put in a dark, cold, lonely hole in the ground. I don't ever want anybody to see the Queen left like that in a cemetery. None of you bastards will ever see me put in the ground." And as it turned out, they didn't.

Somebody said it was just like Dinah to have her own way to the very end.

Dinah Washington did not leave a probatable will. "It was handwritten, in pencil," says LaRue Manns. "It didn't stand up. When she called me from Detroit just before she died, she told me she had written it. She said we were all going to come out there for Christmas and she was going to have the will consummated. She said, 'I'm going to have the lawyer come out here.' And that lawyer was David Dinkins [elected Manhattan Borough President in 1985]. He had just passed the bar, and she'd said, 'I'm gonna give him his first case.' He used to work in his father-in-law's office up there on Saint Nicholas Avenue, and he used to service us. Dinah was crazy about him and his wife, and she wanted to help him.''

But a will written in pencil was not considered legal. Dick "Night Train" Lane, widowed after less than six months of marriage, was now responsible for straightening out Dinah's affairs. "This insurance man called me when he heard she'd died and told me she had a policy he'd talked her into getting. He said, 'I used to go to the Apollo Theater and beg Dinah to take out insurance. What happens if something happens to you out there? What happens if you're in a plane crash? I got a policy—as you put so much money in, even if you stopped paying, got sick, it would pay the policy up. So I finally got her to do it.' He said Dinah's mother was the beneficiary, and I flew her mother to New York, and we turned Ruth's office upside down trying to find that policy. We found it and I said, 'The policy's yours, Mama, you take it; it's your money. Now I'm going back to Detroit, I'm through with it.' She said, 'Dick, what I wanna do is pay the funeral bill and then split it with the kids.' I said, 'You do it.' I go. She calls me up a week later—'I don't know why you're keeping my daughter's stuff. You oughta send it to me, I'm her mother.'

"I told her she had to see Joe Glaser about the fur coats.

Dinah owed Joe Glaser money, and he took all the minks and put them in storage. Whenever she paid so much money, she could get one of the coats out of storage. But I said, 'Mama, you can come over here and get anything you want. But when we went to court and the judge asked, 'Who will take these kids?' you sat there and didn't say a word.'

"I took the kids. They were up in their teens. I took them out of Windsor Mountain and brought them here to Detroit and put them in public school, but the worst thing was trying to get their transcripts, because I hadn't paid the bills. The older boy, George, didn't want to abide by my rules and regulations, so he left. The younger boy stayed. I made him finish high school. I said, 'I promised your mother you would finish high school. You're gonna stay here, no matter how bad you get. He did. During that time I married my son's mother, the girl I jilted for Dinah. She could never forget Dinah, so we didn't stay together that long.''

LaRue Manns thought it was suspicious that Lane married again so soon after Dinah's death. "She hadn't been dead nine months before he was seeing this woman and got married, so that gave me the feeling that he was still hanging on to that one and was just married to Dinah for prestige. But I'm just going by what Dinah mentioned to me and what I saw thereafter and read thereafter.'' Manns never really got to know Lane, and they have not remained in contact.

Manns has limited contact with Dinah's family. Those she sees or hears from most are Ferris Kimbrough, Dinah's stepsister, and George Jenkins, Dinah's elder son, both of whom live in New York, and Bobby Grayson, who lives in Chicago. "They often thought that I got more than I was supposed to get, and they didn't get as much as they were supposed to get, because of me. Because Dinah was good to me. But I didn't get anything. After she died, it occurred to me that I had a couple of furs in with hers in Joe Glaser's storage, but I didn't have the kind of money—say five thousand dollars—to get all those coats out. But Joe told me, 'Anything you want out of here, you come over and get it.' The husband and the mother had gotten to him before it had even occurred to me to get mine out, told him to seal off everything, don't let anybody have anything. I guess they all thought I was going to take everything I could get my hands on. But, hey, it wasn't mine. I only wanted what was for me.

"I didn't even have the money to buy some of the things she had in storage. That was so sad. When she moved to Detroit, she had a lot of things put in storage. It was all auctioned off—and it was beautiful stuff, special made that she'd gotten from a place in Chicago. But like I said, at that time I wasn't able to acquire any of those things. It happened way out in Queens somewhere; the storage people had a place out there."

LaRue Manns later spent six years traveling with Aretha Franklin. She married and divorced. She now works and lives in New York, in the same apartment that Dinah got for her in 1959. She has a few items of clothing and costume jewelry that were Dinah's and cares for them as if they were museum artifacts. She also has a number of treasured photographs and has in the back of her mind the idea of one day publishing this collection of music history.

Ruth Bowen already wrote a book, according to Dick Night Train Lane—an uncomplimentary biography of Dinah Washington. When asked if she'd written a biography of Dinah, however, Bowen said, "Not yet." In 1965, two years after Dinah's death, Bowen changed the name of Queen Artists Corporation to Queen Booking Agency and subsequently formed her own corporation, the Bowen Agency. Over the years, she has represented such clients as Sammy Davis, Jr., Aretha Franklin, Ray Charles, Gladys Knight and the Pips, and Stevie Wonder. She and LaRue Manns are in close contact.

Dinah's mother and Ferris Kimbrough's father have since divorced. Mrs. Alice Jones celebrated her eightieth birthday in the fall of 1985, and it was the occasion for a large family reunion. She says that one of her daughters is going to write a biography of Dinah.

Of Dinah's ex-husbands and ex-quasi-husbands, John Young, George Jenkins, Robert Grayson, Walter Buchanan, and Rafael Campos are either dead or presumed dead. Dick Lane is still in Detroit. Eddie Chamblee was in New York, leading the Eddie Chamblee Quartet in the spring of 1986, but in ill health and thinking of moving to a warmer climate. Jimmy Cobb was happy and healthy with a young family in upstate New York.

Wynton Kelly died in 1970, in Toronto. Says LaRue Manns, "He was so upset when Dinah died. I didn't see Wynton after that because it would have been a catastrophe—carrying on and crying." Keter Betts still lives in the Washington, D.C., area, and has been with Ella Fitzgerald for many years. Jack Wilson is in Los Angeles. Slappy White, Redd Foxx, and Ann Littles live in Las Vegas. Dinah lives in them all.

Dinah Washington's Recordings

Dinah Washington with Lionel Hampton Sextet: Dinah Washington (vcl), acc. by Joe Morris (tp), Rudy Rutherford (cl), Arnett Cobb (ts), Milt Buckner (p), Vernon King (b), Fred Radcliffe (d)

New York, December 29, 1943

LHS1	Evil Gal Blues (3)	Key K605, Tulip 103, Merc MVL300	
LHS2	I Know How to Do It (1)	Key K606	—
LHS3	Salty Papa Blues (3)	—	—
LHS4	Homeward Bound (2)	Key K605	—

NOTE: (1) Lionel Hampton (d) replaces Radcliffe; Lionel Hampton on (2) plays the treble part on piano; on (3) Lionel Hampton plays (vib)

Vcl. acc. by Lucky Thompson's All Stars: Karl George (tp), Jewell Grant (as), Lucky Thompson (ts), Gene Porter (bar), Milt Jackson (vib), Wilbert Baranco (p), Charlie Mingus (b), Lee Young (d)

Los Angeles, December 10, 1945

S1170	Wise Woman Blues	Apollo 368, ABC 27596, Grand Award 33-318
S1171	Walking Woman Blues	Apollo 374

| S1172 | No Voot—No Boot | Apollo 368 |
| S1173 | Chewin' Woman Blues | Apollo 396, ABC 27596, Grand Award 33-318 |

Los Angeles, December 12, 1945

S1174	My Lovin' Papa	Apollo 371
S1175	Rich Man's Blues	Apollo 374, ABC 27596, Grand Award 33-318
S1176	Beggin' Woman Blues	Parrot 20-001, ABC 27596, Grand Award 33-318
S1177	All or Nothing	same issues as S1176

Los Angeles, December 13, 1945

S1178	Mellow Mama Blues	Apollo 371
S1179	My Voot Is Really Vout	Apollo 388
S1180	Blues for a Day	— , ABC 27596, Grand Award 33-318
S1181	Pacific Coast Blues	Apollo 396, —

NOTE: Last four titles of ABC 27596 and Grand Award 33-318 by Betty Roche (vcl), acc. by Earl Hines Sextet

Vcl. acc. by Gus Chappell's Orchestra: Gus Chappell (tb), rest unknown

Chicago, January 1946

201	Embraceable You	Merc MG20119
202	I Can't Get Started	Merc MG20120, 2052
203	When a Woman Loves a Man	Merc 8010
204	Joy Juice	Merc 2052

Vcl. acc. by Gerald Wilson's Orchestra: pers. incl. Gerald Wilson, Snookie Young (tp), Melba Liston (tb), Jimmy Bunn (p), James Robinson (tb), Clyde Dunn, Vernon Slater (ts), Maurice Simon (bar), Henry Green (d)

Los Angeles, 1946

Oo-Wee-Walkie Talkie   Merc 8010

Vcl. acc. by Tab Smith's Orchestra: poss. pers. incl. Frank Galbraith, Russell Royster (tp), Tab Smith (as), Johnny Hicks (ts), Larry Belton (bar), Red Richards (p), Johnny Williams (b), Walter Johnson (d)

New York, 1946

562	A Slick Chick	Merc 8024
563	Postman Blues	—
564	That's When a Woman Loves a Heel	Merc 8030

Vcl. acc. by Chubby Jackson's Orchestra: pers. incl. Chubby Jackson (b) and poss. other members of the Woody Herman Band.

New York, 1946

| 764 | Stairway to the Stars | Merc 8035, MG20119 |
| 765 | I Want to Be Loved | —   — |

Vcl. acc. by Dave Young's Orchestra: Harry Jackson (tp), Andrew Gardner (as), Dave Young (ts), Rudy Martin (p), Bill Settles (b), Curtis Walker (d)

Chicago, 1947

925	You Satisfy	Merc 8102
926	Fool That I Am	—
927	There's Got to Be a Change	—
928	Mean and Evil Blues	—

Vcl. acc. by Rudy Martin's Trio: Rudy Martin (p), Bill Settles (b)

Chicago, 1947

965	Since I Fell for You	Merc 8057, MG20789
966	West Side Baby	Merc 8079, Wing MG12223
967	You Can Depend on Me	Merc 8057
968	Early in the Morning	Merc 8061

Vcl. acc. by Teddy Brannon's Trio: Teddy Brannon (p), unknown g, b, and d

New York, 1947

1148   I Love You, Yes I Do   Merc 8065, Wing MGW12140
1149   Don't Come Knockin'   —   —
       at My Door

Vcl. acc. by Rudy Martin's Trio: Rudy Martin (p), unknown g and b

Chicago, 1947

1225   Walkin' and Talkin'   Merc 8079
1226   Ain't Misbehavin'   Merc 8072
1227   What Can I Say After I Said I'm Sorry   Merc 8133
1228   No More Lonely Gal Blues   Merc 8072

Vcl. acc. by Dave Young's Orchestra: poss. pers. incl. Harry Jackson (tp), Andrew Gardner (as), Dave Young (ts), Rudy Martin (p), Bill Settles (b), Curtis Walker (d)

Chicago, 1947

1266   Tell Me So   Merc 8094
1268   Pete   Merc 8133
1269   Am I Asking Too Much   Merc 8095, MG20119

Vcl. acc. by Cootie Williams Orchestra: Cootie Williams, Bob Merrill (tp), Rupert Cole (as), William Parker (ts), Arnold Jarvis (p), Mundell Lowe (g), Leonard Swain (b), Sonny Payne (d)

New York, 1947

1593-2   Resolution Blues   Merc 8082
1594-2   I Want to Cry   —, MG20119, MG25060
1592   Record Ban Blues   Merc MG20829

Vcl. acc. by unknown cl, p, g, b, and d

New York, 1947

1785   Long John Blues   Merc MG20247, MVL300

Unknown acc.

1824	In the Rain	Merc 8094
1825	I Sold My Heart to the Junkman	Merc 8095, Wing MG12223
1948	I'll Wait	Merc 8107
1950	It's Too Soon to Know	—
2083	Why Can't You Behave	Merc 5521, Wing MGW12223
2084	It's Funny	Merc 8114
2468	Laughing Boy	Merc 8102

Vcl. acc. by Count Basie Orchestra: Clark Terry, Jimmy Nottingham, Harry Edison, Emmett Berry (tp), George Matthews, Bill Johnson, Ted Donnelly, Dickie Wells (tb), Charles Q. Price, Earl Warren (as), Wardell Gray, Paul Gonsalves (ts), Jack Washington (bar), Beryl Booker (p), Freddie Green (g), Gene Wright (b), Shadow Wilson (d)

Broadcast, "Royal Roost," New York,
September 11, 1948

Am I Asking Too Much	Session SR106
Evil Gal Blues	—
I Want to Cry	—

Same location, New York, September 14, 1948

I Want to Cry (unissued)

Vcl. acc. by prob. Dizzy Gillespie Orchestra: prob. Dizzy Gillespie (tp) and others

Same location, New York, October 16, 1948

Am I Asking Too Much (unissued)	
Is It All Too Soon to Know	—
I Want to Cry	—
It Is All Too Soon to Cry	—

Same location, New York, October 23, 1948

Stairway to the Stars (unissued)   —
Evil Gal Blues

Vcl. acc. by Mitch Miller's Orchestra

New York, 1949

2531   Am I Really Sorry   Merc 8150

Vcl. acc. by Teddy Stewart's Orchestra: pers. incl. George Hudson (tp), Rupert Cole, Ernie Wilkins (as), Teddy Stewart (d)

New York, 1949

2825	How Deep Is the Ocean	Merc MG25138, MG20119
2826	New York, Chicago, and Los Angeles	Merc MG25060, Wing MGW12223
2827	Harbor Lights	—
2828	Good Daddy Blues	Merc 8154
2829	Baby Get Lost	Merc MG20247, MVL300
2830	I Only Know	Merc MG25060, MG20119

Vcl. acc. by Mitch Miller's Orchestra

New York, 1949

2874   I Challenge Your Kiss   Merc 8150

Vcl. acc. by Teddy Stewart Orchestra: pers. incl. Teddy Stewart (d) and poss. members of the Dizzy Gillespie Orchestra

New York, 1949

2996	Fast Movin' Mama	Merc 8207
2997	Juice Head Man of Mine	—
2998	Shuckin' and Jivin'	Merc MG20829
2999	Richest Guy in the Graveyard	Merc 8154

Same as above

New York, 1949

3130   Journey's End   Merc 8169

Prob. similar to above

c. 1949–50

3182	It Isn't Fair	Merc MG20119, MG20789
3183	My Kind of Man	Merc 8206
3184	If I Loved You	Merc MG20119, MG20788
3185	Why Don't You Think Things Over	Merc MG20120

Pers. incl. Cecil Payne (bar), Ernie Wilkins (as), Freddie Green (g), Ray Brown (b), Teddy Stewart (d)

New York, 1950

3407	Big Deal	Merc 8187
3408	I'll Never Be Free ✓	— , MG25060, MG20120
3409	I Wanna Be Loved	— MG20119
3410	Love Me with Misery	—

No details

"Just Jazz Concert," Los Angeles, 1950?

Cool Kind Papa	Vogue LDM30220
It Isn't Fair	—
Baby Get Lost	—
I Wanna Be Loved	Vogue LDM30220
Fast Movin' Mama	—

Vcl. acc. by Jimmy Carroll's Orchestra

New York, 1950

3691	Harbor Lights ✓	Merc MG20119, MG20788
3692	I Cross My Fingers ✓	Merc 5488
3693	Time Out for Tears ·	Merc 5503, MG20788
3694	Only a Moment Ago	—

Vcl. acc. by Walter Buchanan's Orchestra: pers. incl. Walter
Buchanan (b)

New York, February 1951

3877	Fine Fine Daddy	Merc 8232
3878	Please Send Me Someone to Love	Merc 8231, Wing MGW12140
3879	Ain't Nobody's Business If I Do	— MGW12223
3880	I'm So Lonely I Could Cry	Merc 8232

Vcl. acc. by Jimmy Carroll's Orchestra

New York, 1951

4041	My Heart Cries for You	Merc MG20120
4042	I Apologize	—
4043	I Won't Cry Anymore	— , MG20479
4044	Don't Say You're Sorry Again	—

Vcl. acc. by Nook Shrier's Orchestra

New York, September 1951

| 4220 | Mixed Emotions | Merc MG20120, MG20788 |
| 4222 | Baby Did Your Hear Me | — |

Vcl. acc. by Ike Carpenter's Orchestra: Clyde Reasinger, Tom
Reeves (tp), Art Pearlman, Roger White (tb), Ed Freeman (as),
Bob Hardaway, Bob Robinson (ts), Joe Koch (bar), Wynton Kelly
(p), Chuck Norris (g), Joe O'Rear (b), Dick Stanton (d)

Los Angeles, June 1, 1951

4367	What's the Matter Baby	Merc MG20829
4368	Don't Hold It Against Me	Merc MG20247, MVL300
4369	Be Fair to Me	Merc 8249
4370	Just One More Chance	Merc MG20120

Ike Carpenter (p) replaces Kelly, Norris out

Los Angeles, June 2, 1951

4371	Get All My Loving on Saturday Night	Merc 8249
4372	If You Don't Think I'm Leaving	Merc 5665
4373	I'm a Fool to Want You	—
4374	I'm Crying Cause You're Laughing at Me	Merc MG20829

Vcl. acc. by the Ravens (vcl group)

New York, October 1951

| 4613 | Out in the Cold Again | Merc 8257, Wing MGW12223 |
| 4614 | Hey Good Lookin' | —   — |

Vcl. acc. by Jimmy Cobb's Orchestra: Ben Webster, Wardell Gray (ts), Wynton Kelly (p), Jimmy Cobb (d), and 9 to 10 others

Los Angeles, c. late December 1951
or early January 1952

4731	Wheel of Fortune	Merc 8267, Wing MGW12223
4732	Tell Me Why	— —
4733	Trouble in Mind	Merc MG20247, MG20439, MVL300
4734	When the Sun Goes Down	Merc MG20829

Vcl. acc. by Walter Rodell's Orchestra: pers. incl. strings Wynton Kelly (p), Keeter Betts (b), Jimmy Cobb (d)

Chicago, March 1952

4896	Mad About the Boy	Merc 5842, MG20788
4897	I Can't Face the Music	—
4898	Stormy Weather	Merc 5906, MG20789

Similar

Chicago, 1952

| 9036 | My Devotion | Merc MG20829 |
| 9037 | Make Believe Dreams | — |

Vcl. acc. incl. Paul Quinichette (ts), Jackie Davis (org), Wynton Kelly (p), Keeter Betts (b), Jimmy Cobb (d)

Chicago, 1952

9220	Pillow Blues	Merc 8292
9221	Cold, Cold Heart	Merc MG25140, MG20120, 20789
9222	Double Dealing Daddy	Merc 8292
9223	New Blowtop Blues	Merc MG20247, MVL300

Vcl. acc. by Jimmy Cobb's Orchestra: pers. incl. Russell Procope (cl, as), Paul Gonsalves (ts), Beryl Booker (p), Keeter Betts (b), Jimmy Cobb (d), Clark Terry (tp)

Chicago, 1952

9247	My Song	Merc 8294
9248	Half as Much	—
9249	I Cried for You	Wing MGW12140
9250	Gambler's Blues	Merc MG20247, MVL300

Vcl. with unknown acc.

9580	You Let My Love Grow Old	Merc 70125
9581	Silent Night	Merc 70263
9582	The Lord's Prayer	—
9583	Ain't Nothing Good	Merc 70125

From unknown session

	Don't Get Around Much Anymore	Merc MG20829

Vcl. acc. by Paul Quinichette (ts), Jackie Davis (org), Candido Camero (bgo), Jimmy Cobb (d), and others

New York, June 1953

9790	Fat Daddy	Merc MG20247
9791	Go Pretty Daddy	Merc MG20829
9792	TV Is the Thing	Merc MG20247
9793	Feel Like I Wanna Cry	Merc MG20119, Wing MGW12140

9794   My Lean Baby   —
9795   Never Never   —

Vcl. acc. by Clark Terry (tp), Gus Chappell (tb), Rick Henderson (as), Eddie Davis, Paul Quinichette (ts), Jackie Davis (org), Junior Mance or Sleepy Anderson (p), Keeter Betts (b), Ed Thigpen (d), Candido Camero (bgo)

New York, June 17, 1953

9870   Am I Blue   EmArcy MG36028
9871   Pennies from Heaven   —

Vcl. with unknown acc.

9920   Set Me Free   Merc MG20829
9921   Since My Man Has Gone and   Merc 70284
          Went
10131 My Man's an Undertaker   Wing MGW12140

Same or similar pers. as June 17, 1953

New York, 1953

10242 Short John   Wing MGW12140
10243 Old Man's Darlin'   Merc MG20829
10244 Love for Sale   EmArcy MG36028
10245 Our Love Is Here to Stay   —

Vcl. with unknown acc.

New York, March 1954

10386 Such a Night   Merc MG20788
10387 Until Sunrise   Merc MG20120
10388 One Arabian Night   Merc MG20829

Same pers. as June 17, 1953, but Quinichette (ts) out

New York, June 15, 1954

10618 I Let a Song Go Out   EmArcy MG26032, MG36028
          of My Heart
10619 A Foggy Day   —   —

| 10620 | Bye Bye Blues | — | — |
| 10621 | Blue Skies | — | — |

Vcl. with unknown acc.

New York, 1954

| 10651 | No You Can't Love Two | Merc 70392 |
| 10654 | Big Long Slidin' Thing | — |

Vcl. acc. by Hal Mooney's Orchestra:

Los Angeles, August 3, 1954

10862	Dream	Merc MG20789, Wing MGW12140
10863	I Don't Hurt Anymore	—	—
10864	Soft Winds	70906
10865	If It's the Last Thing I Do	70600

Vcl. acc. by Clifford Brown, Clark Terry (tp), Junior Mance (p), Keeter Betts (b), Max Roach (d)

Los Angeles, August 14, 1954

| 10901 | I've Got You Under My Skin | EmArcy MG36000 |
| 10902 | No More | — |

Herb Geller (as), Harold Land (ts), same date

| 10905 | You Go to My Head | EmArcy MG36000 |

Maynard Ferguson (tp) added, same date

| 10907 | Lover Come Back to Me | EmArcy MG36000 |
| 10908 | Medley: Alone Together Summertime Come Rain or Come Shine | — |

Junior Mance (p), Keeter Betts (b), Max Roach (d) only, same
date

10910   There Is No Greater Love   EmArcy MG36000

NOTE: For other titles of EmArcy MG36000 see under Jam Session.

Vcl. acc. with unknown big band:

New York, November 1954

11061   Wishing Well   Merc 70497
11062   Teach Me Tonight   — , MG20789
11063   I Just Couldn't Stand It No   Wing MGW12140
               More

Vcl. acc. by prob. Paul Quinichette (ts), Wynton Kelly or Junior
Mance (p), Jimmy Cobb (d)

New York, January 11, 1955

11107   That Is All I Want From   Merc 70537
               You
11108   You Stay on My Mind   — , Wing MGW12140

Vcl. acc. by Clark Terry (tp), Jimmy Cleveland (tb), Paul Quinichette (ts), Cecil Payne (bar), Wynton Kelly (p), Barry Galbraith
(g), Keeter Betts (b), Jimmy Cobb (d), Quincy Jones (arr)

New York, March 15 and 17, 1955

11401   I Could Write a   EmArcy MG36011, Merc MG20574
               Book
11402   Make the Man   —   —
               Love Me
11403   Blue Gardenia   —   —
11404   You Don't   —   —
               Know What
               Love Is

11405	My Old Flame	—	—
11406	Easy Living	—	—
11407	I Get a Kick Out of You	—	—
11408	This Can't Be Love	—	—
11409	A Cottage for Sale	—	—
11410	I Diddle	Merc 70600	
	If I Had You	EmArcy EMS2-401	

Vcl. with unknown acc.

New York, May 1955

11552	I Hear Those Bells	Merc 70652
11554	Let's Get Busy	Merc 70833
11555	The Cheat	Merc 70652
	Not Without You	Merc 70694
	I Concentrate on You	—

New York, September 1955

12086	You Might Have Told Me	Merc 70728
12087	I'm Lost Without You Tonight	—
12088	Let's Go Around Together	Merc 70833

Vcl. acc. by Wynton Kelly (p), Keeter Betts (b), Jimmy Cobb (d), plus strings and Harold Mooney (dir)

Los Angeles, November 10, 1955

12391	Goodbye	EmArcy MG36065, MG36086
12392	The Show Must Go On	Merc 70776
12393	Smoke Gets in Your Eyes	EmArcy MG36065
12394	Look to the Rainbow	—

Vcl. acc. by prob. Maynard Ferguson, Conrad Gozzo, Manny Klein, Ray Linn (tp), Tom Pederson, Frank Rosolino, Si Zentner (tb), Herb Geller, Skeets Herfurt (as), Georgia Auld, Babe Russin (ts), Chuck Gentry (bar), Wynton Kelly (p), Al Hendrickson (g), Keeter Betts (b), Jimmy Cobb (d)

Los Angeles, November 11, 1955

12401	There'll Be Some Changes Made	EmArcy MG36065
12402	I Could Have Told You	—
12403	More Than You Know	—
12404	Make Me a Present of You	—

Same or similar pers.

Los Angeles, November 12, 1955

12417	Ill Wind	EmArcy MG36065
12418	Willow Weep for Me	—
12419	All of Me	—
12420	Accent on Youth	—

Vcl. acc. by Julian "Cannonball" Adderley (as), Junior Mance (p), strings plus others with Hal Mooney (arr, cond)

New York, April 24 and 25, 1956

12874	Let's Do It	EmArcy MG36073
12875	There'll Be a Jubilee	—
12876	Sunny Side of the Street	—
12877	If I Were a Bell	—
12878	I've Got a Crush on You	—
12879	Our Love Is Here to Stay	—
12880	Sometimes I'm Happy	—
12881	Nothing Will Ever Change My Love	—
12882	What Will I Tell My Heart	—
12883	Let Me Love You	—
12884	Say It Isn't So	—
12885	My Ideal	—
12886	Cat on a Hot Tin Roof	Merc 70868
12887	The First Time	—

Vcl. acc. by Quincy Jones's Orchestra: pers. incl. Don Elliott
(tp, vib) Jimmy Cleveland (tb), Anthony Ortega (as)

New York, 1956

13514	Relax Max	Merc 70968
13515	Tears to Burn	Merc 70906
13516	The Kissing Way Home	Merc 70968
13517	I Know	Merc 71043

Vcl. acc. by Ernie Royal, Charlie Shavers, Clark Terry, Joe Wilder (tp), Jimmy Cleveland, Urbie Green, Quentin Jackson (tb),
Tom Mitchell (b-tb), Hal McKusick (as, fl-1), Anthony Ortega
(as), Jerome Richardson, Lucky Thompson (ts), Danny Bank (bar),
Don Elliott (mellophone, vib, xyl-2, tp, bgo), Sleepy Anderson
(p, celeste-3), Barry Galbraith (g), Milt Hinton (b), Jimmy Crawford (d)

New York, October 1956

14382	To Love and Be Loved	Merc 71018
14383	All Because of You	—
14385	You Let My Love Grow Old	Merc 71043
14386	Somebody Loves Me	EmArcy MG36104
14387	Perdido	—
14388	Caravan	—
14389	Is You Is or Is You Ain't My Baby (1)	—

Bernie Glow, Nick Travis (tp), Osie Johnson (d) replace Royal,
Wilder, and Crawford

New York, November 1956

14390	They Didn't Believe Me	EmArcy MG36104
14391	But Not for Me	—
14392	You're Cryin'	—
14393	Ev'ry Time We Say Goodbye	—

Jimmy Maxwell, Doc Severinsen (tp), replace Glow and Travis

New York, November 1956

14394	I'll Close My Eyes (3)	EmArcy MG36104
14395	Makin' Whoopee (2)	—
14396	Never Let Me Go	—

Vcl. with unknown acc.

| 14912 | I'm Gonna Keep My Eye on You | Merc 71087 |
| | Ain't Nobody Home | — |

Vcl. acc. by Ernie Wilkins Orchestra: Reunald Jones, Charlie Shavers, Doc Severinsen, Clark Terry, Ernie Royal, Ray Copeland (tp), Julian Priester, Jimmy Cleveland, Sonny Russo, Rod Levitt (tb), Jerome Richardson (fl, as), Sahib Shihab (as), Benny Golson, Frank Wess, Eddie Chamblee (ts), Charlie Davis (bar), Jack Wilson (p), Richard Evans (b), Charlie Persip (d), Ernie Wilkins (dir, arr)

New York, 1957

15943	Honeysuckle Rose	EmArcy MG36119
15944	Ain't Misbehavin'	—
15947	I've Got a Feelin' I'm Fallin'	—
15948	Keepin' Out of Mischief Now	—
15954	Everybody Loves My Baby	EmArcy MG36119
15955	Blues Up and Down	—
15956	Black and Blue	—
16104	Bad Luck	Merc MG20439
16105	Honk Tonk	Merc 71389
16106	All of Me	Merc MG20439
16107	Light	—
16108	Somewhere Along the Line	Merc 71389, MG20439
16109	Make Me a Present of You	Merc MG20439
16110	Backwater Blues	—
16241	Christopher Columbus	EmArcy MG36119
16242	T' Ain't Nobody's Business	—

16243	Everybody's Rockin' My Dream-boat	—
16244	Jitterbug Waltz	—
16245	Ain't Cha Glad?	—
16246	Squeeze Me	—

Vcl. acc. by Eddie Chamblee's Orchestra: Clark Terry or Fip Ricard (tp), Quentin Jackson (tb), Eddie Chamblee (ts), Gene Easton (bar), James Craig (p), Robert Edmondson (b), James Slaughter (d)

Chicago, December 30, 1957

16709	Trombone Cholly	EmArcy MG36130, Merc 6336328
16710	Send Me to the 'Lectric Chair	—
16711	Careless Love	—

Fip Ricard (tp), Julian Priester (tb), Eddie Chamblee (ts), Charlie Davis (bar), Jack Wilson (p), Robert Edmondson (b, arr), James Slaughter (d)

Chicago, January 7, 1958

16729	Me and My Gin	EmArcy MG36130, Merc 6336328
16730	Jailhouse Blues	—
16731	You've Been a Good Old Wagon	—
16732	After You've Gone (re arr)	—

Ernie Wilkins (arr), rest same

Chicago, January 20, 1958

16975	Black Water Blues	EmArcy MG36130, Merc 6336328
16976	If I Could Be With You	—
16978	Fine Fat Daddy (Ernie Wilkins arr)	—

No details

	Never Again	Merc 71317
	Ring-a My Phone	—

Vcl. acc. by Blue Mitchell (tp), Melba Liston (tb), Harold Ousley (ts), Sahib Shihab (bar), Wynton Kelly (p), Paul West (b), Max Roach (d)

Newport Jazz Festival, July 6, 1958

17638	Lover Come Back to Me	EmArcy MG36141
17639	Crazy Love	—
17640	Back Water Blues	—

Dinah Washington (vcl, vib), acc. by the Terry Gibbs Sextet: Don Elliott (vib, mel), Urbie Green (tb), Terry Gibbs (vib), Wynton Kelly (p), Paul West (b), Max Roach (d)

Newport, R.I., July 5, 1958

17643	All of Me	EmArcy MG36141

NOTE: For more titles, see under Terry Gibbs.

Dinah Washington (vcl), acc. by Belford Hendricks Orchestra

1959

18189	I Won't Cry Anymore	Merc MG20479, MG20789	
18190	What a Diff'rence a Day Made	—	71435
18192	Come on Home		—
18408	Cry Me a River	Merc MG20479	
18409	That's All There Is to That	—	
18410	It's Magic	—	
18411	It Could Happen to You	Merc 71560	
18412	Time After Time	Merc MG20479	
18817	I Thought About You	Merc MG20439, MG20479	

18818	Unforgettable	MG20572, MG20789
18819	When I Fall in Love	—
18820	I'm Through with Love	Merc MG20479
18821	A Sunday Kind of Love	— , MG20439
18822	Alone	Merc MG20572
18848	Manhattan	Merc MG20479
18849	I Remember You	—
18850	Nothing in the World	—

Brook Benton (vcl-1) added

18863	Baby You've Got What It Takes (1)	Merc MG20588, MG20581
18864	I Do (1)	
19043	The Song Is Ended	Merc MG20572, MG20604
19100	I Understand	—
19101	This Love of Mine	—

Brook Benton (vcl-1) added

19222	The Light	Merc MG20439
19223	Ask a Woman Who Knows	Merc MG20572
19225	A Man Only Does	—
19226	Bad Case of the Blues	—
19227	This I Promise You (1)	Merc MG20588
19228	Crazy Love	Merc MG20604
19229	Somewhere Along the Line	Merc MG20439
19230	The Age of Miracles	—

19313	Ole Santa	Merc 71557
19314	Everybody Loves Some-body	Merc MG20572
19393	This Bitter Earth	— , MG20788

Brook Benton (vcl-1) added

19772	There Goes My Heart (1)	Merc MG20588
19773	Daybreak	Merc MG20604
19774	Love Walked In (1)	Merc MG20588
19776	I Got It Bad	Merc MG20604

19777   Lord, You Made Us   —
          Human
19778   Good Morning Heartache   —
Only Brook Benton (vcl)

          Not One Step Behind   Merc MG20588
          (bb vcl)
          Call Me (bb vcl)
          Because of Everything
          (bb vcl)

Vcl. acc. by different orchestras directed by Fred Norman, Nat Goodman, and Belford Hendricks, respectively

1960

19850	I'm in Heaven Tonight	Merc 71696
19851	Show Me the Way	Merc MG20604
19852	While We're Young	—
19853	Lookin' Back	Merc 71744
19854	Again	Merc MG20588
19856	Rockin' Good Way (1)	—
19857	I Believe	—
20179	Misery	Merc MG20604
20182	I Concentrate on You	—
20183	Fool That I Am	—
20184	Forgotten	—
20525	We Have Love	Merc 71744
20526	You've Got Me Crying Again	Merc MG20614
20527	The Sun Forgot to Shine	—
20528	Early Every Morning	Merc 71778
20529	Hurt	Merc MG20614
20530	Out of Sight Out of Mind	—
20531	Don't Let the Sun Catch You Cryin'	—
20532	Harbour Lights	— , MG20788
20533	Stardust	—

20534	You Taught Me	—
20535	I'll Never Kiss You Goodbye	Merc MG20638
20536	It Shouldn't Happen to a Dream	Merc MG20614
20537	I Wish I Didn't Love You So	—
20639	Laugh or Cry	Merc MG20614
20640	I Remember Clifford	Merc MG20439
20641	I'll Come Back for More	Merc MG20638
20642	Do You Want It That Way	—
20643	September in the Rain	— , MG20788
20644	Tell Love Hello	—
20645	Don't Go to Strangers	Merc MG20614
	Show Time	Merc MG20439

c. 1961

20809	Without a Song	Merc MG20638
20810	With a Song in My Heart	—
20823	This Heart of Mine	Merc MG20638
20824	Softly	—
20825	Our Love Is Here to Stay	Merc MG20651
20826	Congratulations to Someone	—
20827	As Long as I'm in Your Arms	Merc MG20638
20828	I Can't Believe That You're in Love with Me	Merc MG20638
20829	I've Got My Love to Keep Me Warm	Merc MG20638
20830	I Was Telling Him About You	—

Vcl. acc. by Ernie Freeman (p), Barney Kessel, Rene Hall (g), Red Callender (b), Earl Palmer (d), plus strings and Belford Hendricks (arr, cond)

Los Angeles, January 1961

Love Is a Many-Splendored Thing	Merc MG21119, MVL309	
An Affair to Remember	—	—
Cabin in the Sky	—	—
Pagan Love Song	—	—
Blue Skies	—	—
Three Coins in the Fountain	—	—
Stormy Weather	—	—
Love Letters	—	—
On Green Dolphin Street	—	—
Six Bridges to Cross	—	—

Vcl. acc. by orchestra directed by Quincy Jones

1961

21151	Don't Explain	Merc MG20729
21152	In the Wee Small Hours of the Morning	Merc MG20661
21153	Blue Gardenia	Merc MG20729
21154	Bewitched	Merc MG20661
21155	Am I Blue	—
21156	Everybody's Somebody's Fool	Merc MG20729

Vcl. acc. by Joe Newman (tp), Billy Byers (tb), Al Cohn (ts), and others

21163	If I Should Lose You	Merc MG20661
21165	Wake the Town and Tell the People	—
21175	You Do Something to Me	—
21176	Jeepers Creepers	—
21178	Secret Love	—
21243	Invitation	Merc MG20729
21330	Mood Indigo	Merc MG20661
21331	God Bless the Child	Merc MG20729
21332	I'm a Fool to Want You	Merc MG20661
21333	A Stranger in Town	Merc MG20729

21334	Sometimes I'm Happy	—
21335	Let's Fall in Love	—
21336	I Just Out About Love	Merc MG20661
22020	When Your Lover Has Gone	Merc MG20729
23054	Tears and Laughter	Merc MG20661
23055	I Can't Face the Music	Merc MG20729

Vcl. acc. by orchestra directed by Quincy Jones: pers. incl. Joe Newman (tp), Billy Byers (tb), and others

Chicago, December 1961

23155	Since I Fell for You	Merc MG20789
23156	Dream	—
23157	Such a Night	Merc MG20788
23158	Salty Papa Blues	—
23159	It Don't Hurt Anymore	Merc MG20789
23160	Trust in Me	Merc MG20788
23162	Tell Me Why	Merc MG20789
23163	It Isn't Fair	—
23164	Time Out for Tears	Merc MG20788
23167	Mad About the Boy	—
23168	Mixed Emotions	—
23169	I Wanna Be Loved	— , MG20729
23170	Make Believe Dreams	Merc MG20789
23172	Stormy Weather	Merc MG20789
23173	You're Crying	Merc MG20729

Vcl. acc. by orchestra under dir. of Fred Norman

New York, 1962

16696	You're Nobody Till Somebody Loves You	Roulette R25170
16699	Where Are You	—
	Is You Is or Is You Ain't My Baby	—
	Take Your Shoes Off Baby	—
	Drinking Again	—
	Destination Moon	—

Miss You   —
A Handful of Stars   —
Red Sails in the Sunset   —
Coquette   —

Vcl. acc. by orchestra dir. by Don Costa: incl. strings

1962

You're a Sweetheart   Roulette R25180
Fly Me to the Moon   —
Our Love   —
Love Is the Sweetest Thing   —
I'll Close My Eyes   —
I Didn't Know About You   —
If It's the Last Thing I Do   —
Do Nothin' Till You Hear From Me   —
My Devotion   —
That's My Desire   —
Was It Like That?   —
Me and the One I Love   —

Vcl. with unknown acc.

c. 1962–63

He's Gone Again   Bellaphon (G)BLST6533

Vcl. acc. by orchestra dir. by Don Costa

New York, 1962–63

16729   For All We Know   Roulette R25183
         Just Friends   —
         I'm Gonna Laugh You Out of My   —
            Life
         I'll Be Around   —
         Lament (Love I Found You)   —
         I Don't Know You Anymore   —
         Baby Won't You Please Come   —
            Home

	Lover Man	—
	The Man That Got Away	—
	Say It Isn't So	—
	On the Street of Regret	—

Vcl. acc. by orchestra dir. by Fred Norman: Ernie Royal, Joe Newman, Marky Markowitz (tp), Morton Bullman, Robert Ascher, Chauncey Welsh (tb), Bill Rame, George Benz, Gerald Satini (ts, as), Eddie Chamblee (ts), Cecil Payne (bar), Wynton Kelly (p), Billy Butler, Carl Lynch (g), Milt Hinton (b), Panama Francis (d), E. Maxwell (harp), strings-1, background vcl-2

1963

16860	I Wouldn't Know	Roulette 4444
16861	No Hard Feelings (1,2)	Roulette R25189
	If I Never Get to Heaven	—
	The Blues Ain't Nothing but a Woman	—
	Nobody Knows the Way I Feel This Morning	—
	You've Been a Good Old Wagon	—
	It's a Mean Old Man's World (1)	—
	How Long, How Long Blues (1)	—
	Don't Come Running Back to Me	—
	Key to the Highway (2)	Roulette R25189
	Duck Before You Drown	—
17166	Romance in the Dark	—
17129	Let Me Be the First to Know	—
17307	Soulville	Roulette R25253

same pers.

1963

	I Wanna Be Around	Roulette R25220
	Make Someone Happy	—
	Rags to Riches	—
	Take Me in Your Arms	—
	I'll Drown in my Tears	—

Why Was I Born	—
I Left My Heart in San Francisco	—
The Show Must Go On	—
I'm Glad for Your Sake	—
There Must Be a Way	—
What Kind of Fool Am I?	—
Bill	—

Vcl. acc by orchestra dir. by Fred Norman and Marty Manning with strings and vcl. choir

1963

That Sunday	Roulette R25244
I've Run Out of Reasons	—
Something's Gotta Give	—
Funny Thing	—
They Said You Came Back Running	—
Lingering	—
The Good Life	—
Start Over My Shoulder	—
Icy Stone	—
Call Me Irresponsible	—
Make Believe Dreams	—
Lord You Made Us Human	—

The following belong into the above Roulette sessions

Drown in My Own Tears	Roulette R25253
My and My Gin	—
Stranger on Earth	—

Vcl. acc. by large orchestra with strings, org., Don Costa (arr)

1963

What's New	Roulette (S)R25269
I'll Never Stop Loving You	—
He's My Guy	—

To Forget About You	—
Somebody Else Is Taking My Place	—
That Old Feeling	—
He's Gone Again	—
These Foolish Things	—
Me and My Gin	—
Just One More Chance ✓	—
Don't Say Nothin' at All	—

-The finer Dinah-: Vcl. with unknown acc.

Ain't Misbehavin' ✓	Harlem HHP-8002
I Cried for You ✓	—
Willow Weep for Me ✓	—
What a Difference a Day Made ✓	—
This Bitter Earth ✓	—
Unforgettable ✓	—
Baby	—
Teach Me Tonight ✓	Harlem HHP-8002
Stormy Weather ✓	—

Index